Islamophobia

Other Books in the Current Controversies Series

Islamophobia

Dedria Bryfonski, Book Editor

GREENHAVEN PRESS
A part of Gale, Cengage Learning

GALE
CENGAGE Learning·

Detroit • New York • San Francisco • New Haven, Conn • Waterville, Maine • London

Elizabeth Des Chenes, *Director, Publishing Solutions*

© 2013 Greenhaven Press, a part of Gale, Cengage Learning

Gale and Greenhaven Press are registered trademarks used herein under license.

For more information, contact:
Greenhaven Press
27500 Drake Rd.
Farmington Hills, MI 48331-3535
Or you can visit our Internet site at gale.cengage.com

Articles in Greenhaven Press anthologies are often edited for length to meet page requirements. In addition, original titles of these works are changed to clearly present the main thesis and to explicitly indicate the author's opinion. Every effort is made to ensure that Greenhaven Press accurately reflects the original intent of the authors. Every effort has been made to trace the owners of copyrighted material.

Cover image copyright © Tony Savino/Corbis.

LIBRARY OF CONGRESS CATALOGING-IN-PUBLICATION DATA

Islamophobia / Dedria Bryfonski, book editor.
p. cm. -- (Current controversies)
Includes bibliographical references and index.
ISBN 978-0-7377-6235-8 (hardcover) -- ISBN 978-0-7377-6236-5 (pbk.)
1. Islam--Public opinion. 2. Islamophobia. 3. War on Terrorism, 2001-2009. 4. Muslims--Non-Muslim countries. 5. Islam in mass media. I. Bryfonski, Dedria.
BP52.I853 2012
305.6'97--dc23
2012024246

Printed in the United States of America
1 2 3 4 5   16 15 14 13 12

FD296

Contents

J. Mark Halstead

There are four distinct forms of Islamophobia—pre-reflective personal Islamophobia, which discriminates against Muslims simply because they have different beliefs; post-reflective personal Islamophobia, which justifies discrimination on the basis that Muslim beliefs and practices are inferior; institutional Islamophobia, which occurs when Western institutions simply ignore the cultural and religious differences of Muslims when setting policy; and political Islamophobia, which occurs when politicians deliberately portray Muslims as a threat to the West for their own political benefit.

Arthur F. Buehler

A partisan segment of the mass media contributes to the spread of Islamophobia by deliberately portraying Islam as a religion of violence. Islam is described as being profoundly different from western religions and values and therefore dangerous.

Wajahat Ali et al.

An investigation by the Center for American Progress Action Fund revealed that the misinformation stoking Islamophobia in the United States is not broad-based but rather originates with five pseudo-experts whose work is funded by seven foundations. The misinformation they spawn is spread by a number of conservative media outlets and echoed by some right-wing politicians.

Chapter 2: Is America Islamophobic?

Yes: America Is Islamophobic

The July 2011 terrorist attack in Norway by a right-wing extremist could just as well have happened in the United States, because Islamophobia is rampant here.

Islamophobia Has Replaced Anti-Semitism in the United States

Nadine Epstein

Since September 11, 2001, Muslim Americans are having a harder time finding a job, are more likely to face discrimination on the job, and are more likely to lose their security clearances. Although anti-Semitism was prevalent in the 1940s and 1950s, it has virtually disappeared today, with Islamophobia taking its place.

Bigots Are Responsible for the Spread of Islamophobia to Mainstream Americans

Mosharraf Zaidi

Such racist extremists as Newt Gingrich, Pamela Geller, and Terry Jones are exaggerating the threat posed by the Muslim religion and spreading Islamophobia to mainstream Americans. Otherwise decent people are accepting these lies, in part because of the anxieties caused by the perilous economic condition in the United States.

Anti-Muslim Sentiment Is a Problem on College Campuses

Akbar Ahmed and Lawrence Rosen

The proliferation of classes on terrorism and security studies in universities has contributed to Islamophobia, since many professors focus on the violent aspects of Islam. Various strategies are available to faculty who seek to facilitate open discussion on Islam and American Muslims.

No: America Is Not Islamophobic

Anti-Muslim Bigotry Is Exaggerated

Russ Smith

Although some anti-Muslim sentiment does exist in the United States, it is nowhere near the level claimed by such left-leaning commentators as Peter Beinart, who compare the discrimination against Muslims today to the Joseph McCarthy witch hunts of communists in the 1940s and 1950s.

Chapter 3: Is Suspicion of Islam Rational?

Both conservatives and liberals have valid arguments supporting their views on Islam. Conservatives are correct in saying that Islamic fundamentalists have vowed to destroy western society and that several Muslim nations harshly punish their citizens for what the West would perceive as minor offenses. Liberals are correct that right-wing politicians and activists, by claiming that the Islam religion is fundamentally violent and that all Muslims are to be feared, are responsible for the spread of Islamophobia.

Yes: Suspicion of Islam Is Rational

No: Suspicion of Islam Is Not Rational

Irrational fears often have their roots in centuries-old events. Islamophobia is an irrational fear, and it is connected in the West to the ways the medieval Crusades were described in literature.

Chapter 4: Does Sharia Law Pose a Threat to America?

Sharia Law is sexist, exacts harsh punishments for minor offenses, and violates civil rights. As an example, under Sharia Law a man is allowed to rape and abuse his wife.

No: Sharia Law Does Not Pose a Threat to America

Foreword

By definition, controversies are "discussions of questions in which opposing opinions clash" (*Webster's Twentieth Century Dictionary Unabridged*). Few would deny that controversies are a pervasive part of the human condition and exist on virtually every level of human enterprise. Controversies transpire between individuals and among groups, within nations and between nations. Controversies supply the grist necessary for progress by providing challenges and challengers to the status quo. They also create atmospheres where strife and warfare can flourish. A world without controversies would be a peaceful world; but it also would be, by and large, static and prosaic.

The Series' Purpose

The purpose of the Current Controversies series is to explore many of the social, political, and economic controversies dominating the national and international scenes today. Titles selected for inclusion in the series are highly focused and specific. For example, from the larger category of criminal justice, Current Controversies deals with specific topics such as police brutality, gun control, white collar crime, and others. The debates in Current Controversies also are presented in a useful, timeless fashion. Articles and book excerpts included in each title are selected if they contribute valuable, long-range ideas to the overall debate. And wherever possible, current information is enhanced with historical documents and other relevant materials. Thus, while individual titles are current in focus, every effort is made to ensure that they will not become quickly outdated. Books in the Current Controversies series will remain important resources for librarians, teachers, and students for many years.

In addition to keeping the titles focused and specific, great care is taken in the editorial format of each book in the series. Book introductions and chapter prefaces are offered to provide background material for readers. Chapters are organized around several key questions that are answered with diverse opinions representing all points on the political spectrum. Materials in each chapter include opinions in which authors clearly disagree as well as alternative opinions in which authors may agree on a broader issue but disagree on the possible solutions. In this way, the content of each volume in Current Controversies mirrors the mosaic of opinions encountered in society. Readers will quickly realize that there are many viable answers to these complex issues. By questioning each author's conclusions, students and casual readers can begin to develop the critical thinking skills so important to evaluating opinionated material.

Current Controversies is also ideal for controlled research. Each anthology in the series is composed of primary sources taken from a wide gamut of informational categories including periodicals, newspapers, books, US and foreign government documents, and the publications of private and public organizations. Readers will find factual support for reports, debates, and research papers covering all areas of important issues. In addition, an annotated table of contents, an index, a book and periodical bibliography, and a list of organizations to contact are included in each book to expedite further research.

Perhaps more than ever before in history, people are confronted with diverse and contradictory information. During the Persian Gulf War, for example, the public was not only treated to minute-to-minute coverage of the war, it was also inundated with critiques of the coverage and countless analyses of the factors motivating US involvement. Being able to sort through the plethora of opinions accompanying today's major issues, and to draw one's own conclusions, can be a complicated and frustrating struggle. It is the editors' hope that Current Controversies will help readers with this struggle.

Introduction

"Although animosity toward Muslims escalated after the attacks of September 11, 2001, it has much deeper roots."

*I*slamophobia is defined as a prejudice against or fear of Islam and Muslims. The term itself is controversial. Critics of the term argue that the word *phobia* denotes an irrational fear and that it is not irrational to be afraid of Muslims. Additionally, they contend that the term is used to stifle legitimate criticism of Islam. However, the term has become widely used. In their 2007 book *Islamophobia: Making Muslims the Enemy*, Peter Gottschalk and Gabriel Greenberg suggest that "'Islamophobia' accurately reflects a *social* anxiety towards Islam and Muslim cultures that is largely unexamined by, yet deeply ingrained in, Americans."

Although animosity toward Muslims escalated after the attacks of September 11, 2001, it has much deeper roots. The tension between Christians and Muslims dates back to the seventh century with the founding of the Muslim religion. Arthur F. Buehler, in his article "Islamophobia: A Projection of the West's 'Dark Side'," states:

> Islam and its followers became a new religio-political enemy for the Christians after most of the Middle East and North Africa, which had been under Christian Byzantine control, had come under Muslim rule in the seventh and eighth centuries. . . . Islam as the 'religion of the sword' and 'the enemy other' appears to be deeply embedded both in Christendom's and the modern West's collective cultural consciousness.

As more and more Middle Eastern areas, including the city of Jerusalem, came under Muslim rule, tensions between

Christians and Muslims escalated and resulted in a series of nine wars, called the Crusades, that stretched from the end of the eleventh century through the thirteenth century. The Crusades began as a conflict over possession of the Holy Lands. As time went on, Christian objectives expanded to include reclaiming Spain from the Moors. Karen Armstrong in *Holy War* writes:

> The Crusades ... were not wholly rational movements that could be explained away by purely economic or territorial ambition or by the clash of rights and interests. They were fueled, on all sides, by myths and passions that were far more effective in getting people to act than any purely political motivation.

One result of the Crusades was the deterioration of relations between Muslims and Christians—a distrust that continues to the present day.

The term *Islamophobia* apparently was first used in the 1980s and first appeared in print in February 1991, in an article about Russian activities in Afghanistan in the magazine *Insight on the News*. The concept became more widely used following an influential report published by the British think tank Runnymede Trust in 1997 titled *Islamophobia: A Challenge for Us All*. The report states:

> The word 'Islamophobia' has been coined because there is a new reality that needs naming: anti-Muslim prejudice has grown so considerably and so rapidly in recent years that a new item in the vocabulary is needed so that it can be identified and acted against.

The report makes a distinction between open and closed views of Islam, labeling criticism that represents a closed view of Islam as Islamophobic.

The terrorist attacks on September 11, 2001, intensified Islamophobia, particularly in the United States. In 2002, the Federal Bureau of Investigation reported a sharp increase in the number of hate crimes against Muslims in the United States. Robert Steinbeck stated in the Southern Poverty Law Center's Summer 2011 *Intelligence Report*:

> The American public psyche has undergone a subtle but profound metamorphosis since 2001, moving from initial rage at the 9/11 mass murder to fear of another devastating attack by Muslim extremists to, most recently, a more generalized fear of Islam itself. That evolution from specific concerns to general stereotyping is the customary track of racism and xenophobia—and in Muslims, those inclined to bigotry may have found their perfect bogeyman.

In *Current Controversies: Islamophobia,* the viewpoints of various writers are presented in the following chapters: What Factors Contribute to Islamophobia? Is America Islamophobic? Is Suspicion of Islam Rational? and Does Sharia Law Pose a Threat to America?

CHAPTER 1

What Factors Contribute to Islamophobia?

Overview:
There Are Four Distinct
Forms of Islamophobia

J. Mark Halstead

J. Mark Halstead is head of the Department of Community and International Education at the University of Huddersfield in the United Kingdom.

The term *Islamophobia* is a neologism dating from the early 1990s, constructed by analogy with terms such as *agoraphobia* [fear of being in public places], *xenophobia* [fear of foreign people and their cultures], and *homophobia* [fear of homosexuals]. Islamophobia denotes a range of negative feelings toward Muslims and their religion, from generalized bigotry, intolerance, and prejudice on the one hand to a morbid dread and hatred on the other. It may manifest itself in an equally broad range of negative actions and responses, including discrimination against Muslims, social exclusion, verbal and physical harassment, hate crimes, attacks on mosques, and vilification of Islam in the media. . . .

Pre-Reflective Personal Islamophobia

Four main kinds of Islamophobia can be identified. The first of these is *pre-reflective personal Islamophobia*. This involves prejudice and discrimination against Muslims simply because they have different beliefs and values and is embodied in the phrase, "Why can't they be more like us?" Such prejudice may have deep roots, which some psychologists consider fundamental to human personality, including motivational dispositions such as rejection, aggression, dominance, and superior-

J. Mark Halstead, "Islamophobia," *Encyclopedia of Race, Ethnicity, and Society*, Vol. 2, pp. 762–764. Thousand Oaks, CA: Sage Publications, 2008. Copyright © 2008 by Sage Publications. All rights reserved. Reproduced by permission.

ity, and the tendency to feel fear, insecurity, and suspicion in the presence of people who are perceived as strange, foreign, or unfamiliar. It may also be related to ignorance of Muslim beliefs and values, which may leave people open to an uncritical acceptance of myths about Islam.

From these roots, Islamophobic attitudes can easily develop that are extremely difficult to change by argument or the presentation of facts. The attitudes may be kept hidden or expressed openly and may be directed toward all Muslims or toward an individual because he or she is Muslim. The attitudes are likely to be expressed in hostile behavior that includes blaming all Muslims for terrorist attacks, defacing mosques and Muslim graves, and ripping the *hijabs* [traditional head covering for Muslim women] from women's heads, along with rudeness, threats, verbal abuse, spitting, bullying, attacks on property, violence, and murder. Islamophobia also includes the avoidance of social contact with Muslims (even to the extent of refusing to fly in the same aircraft as a Muslim) and discrimination against them in employment, housing, and other areas of social contact. There is strong evidence to suggest that the less dramatic manifestations of pre-reflective personal Islamophobia form part of the everyday experience of many Muslims in the West and that its more dramatic manifestations are commonly perceived as real threats.

Politicians have frequently played on Islamophobic attitudes to increase their popularity.

Post-Reflective Personal Islamophobia

The second form of Islamophobia is *post-reflective personal Islamophobia*. In this form, the hostile attitudes and behavior are more conscious and intentional. Prejudice and discrimination against Muslims are justified by the claim that Islamic values are inferior to the liberal values of the West. Islamic education is dismissed as indoctrination, and evidence of the inferiority of Islamic values is found in the "fanatical" Muslim protests against freedom of speech (for example, against [Salman Rushdie's novel] *The Satanic Verses* or the Danish Jyllands-Posten cartoons that depicted the Prophet Muhammad as a terrorist) and the "oppression" of Muslim women symbolized in the *hijab* and the burqa [enveloping outer garment worn by Muslim women]. Journalists have often led this righteous crusade, legitimizing and giving credibility to hatred and prejudice against Islam, and these attitudes are further reinforced through the exaggerated stereotypes of Muslims in films such as *The Siege, Aladdin,* and *Raiders of the Lost Ark.*

Institutional Islamophobia

The third kind is *institutional Islamophobia*. This occurs where certain practices that disadvantage Muslims in the West are built into social institutions and structures, and no attempt is made to remove them as long as the balance of power lies in the hands of non-Muslims. The practices may be existing ones or new policies, but the key factor is that they ignore the needs and wishes of Muslims. An example is dress codes that are not necessary for health and safety reasons but that put Muslims in a position where they are expected to act in a way that contravenes the requirements of their faith. Other examples might be setting public examinations on important Islamic festivals like *Eid al-Fitr* or *Eid al-Adha*, denying opportunities for Muslim workers to pray at the workplace in accordance with the requirements of their faith, or insisting that no sacred texts other than the Bible can be used when witnesses are sworn in for testimony in court. The assumption in the West that all religions are like Christianity may also result in institutionalized practices that disadvantage Muslims, especially assumptions that faith is a matter of individual choice and that individuals should be free to interpret their faith in the light of their own understanding.

Political Islamophobia

The fourth kind is *political Islamophobia*. Politicians have frequently played on Islamophobic attitudes to increase their popularity. Policies such as the banning of conspicuous religious symbols in schools in France have also been condemned as Islamophobic, especially when they have led to the expulsion of girls wearing Muslim headscarves from school. Attempts to counter the threat of terrorism in the aftermath of the September 11th attacks have had a disproportionate impact on the lives of Muslims in the West: Muslims are more likely than other groups to be stopped by the police, to be targeted in antiterrorist raids, to be accused of not being fully committed to citizenship in the West, and to be spied on in universities and other institutions as potential terrorist suspects.

Political Islamophobia is the most controversial of the four kinds because politicians can always claim that they are representing the views of their constituents and also because the line is not always clear between the legitimate self-protection of a country from terrorist attacks and the illegitimate targeting and harassment of an entire religious group because of the activities of a tiny minority within that group. However, some scholars have concluded that the whole concept of Islamophobia is controversial, and have dismissed it as a myth or a form of intellectual blackmail. They argue that the term is unhelpful in the complex context of Muslim minorities in the West because the onus is on Muslims themselves to adopt the dominant public values of the society in which they live. These scholars claim that the term *Islamophobia* is being used to deflect and silence legitimate critical scrutiny of Islam and its values. From this view, the Danish cartoons should not be considered as Islamophobic, but as an example of a long-standing Western tradition of satire, and raising issues such as wearing the veil as a matter for debate is not Islamophobic but, rather, a necessary approach in a liberal, multicultural society. Claiming that Islamophobia is responsible for the low achievement of Muslim students is also dismissed as an excuse; students should accept responsibility for their own levels of achievement.

Though the term may sometimes be misapplied to anything that Muslims do not like, fear, hatred, and prejudice toward Muslims are widespread in the contemporary Western world, and treating these views and emotional responses as natural or as necessarily the fault of the Muslims themselves (because they refuse to change their own beliefs and values) is not a helpful response. States and organizations that claim to base their practices on justice, equality, and freedom must be willing to review policies and procedures to avoid discrimination against, and promote equal opportunities for, Muslims and to ensure that harassment and hostility are not part of the daily experience of Muslims living in the West.

The Mass Media Contributes to the Spread of Islamophobia

Arthur F. Buehler

Arthur F. Buehler is a senior lecturer at Victoria University in Wellington, New Zealand.

The mass media, if not a contributing factor to islamophobia, is surely the vector that communicates the phobia. Although technically the mass media is quite diverse, overall there are some common characteristics. By depicting horrific scenes from all over the world, it is an ideal means to instill fear in large populations, especially in countries where the average household watches television eight hours a day. Michael Sells poignantly sums up the effects of mass media manipulation:

> Images of Taliban students sitting above the written text of the Qur'an allegedly 'studying the Qur'an' (when actually they are studying intense political indoctrination), or of [Osama] Bin Laden surrounded by Arabic script and Islamic symbols, are shown repeatedly by the media, interspliced with pictures of the planes flying into the [World Trade Center] Towers or other horrors, and with the human suffering of the victims and their relatives and survivors. Once that image-association is made, all the pontifications about how all Muslims are not Taliban [Islamic political and military group] are as effective as pontifications on the dangers of cigarette smoking after someone has ingested thousands of images of smokers as Marlboro man, Sexy man, Sophisticate Woman, Liberated Woman. Once someone has seen the image association of mass-killer (Saddam [Hussein], Bin Laden), Islamic symbol (written Qur'an, Muslims praying,

sounds of the call to prayer) and atrocity (towers burning and collapsing, relatives of victims in anguish), it becomes extraordinarily difficult, however much one tries, to hear and listen to the voices of the vast world of Islam beyond such fanaticism.

The Mass Media Spreads Negative Images of Muslims

The globalised mass media, financed and controlled by vested interests, contributes directly to islamophobia, capitalising on conflicts in the Islamic world to spread negative images and fear of Muslims. The kind of hate speech directed against Islam and Muslims would never be tolerated if it were focused against any other religious group. The Western mass media effectively legitimise islamophobic attitudes in the name of 'free speech'.

From a European perspective, Islam was 'the religion of the sword'.

An almost exclusive mass-media focus has been placed on what has come to be labelled as political, militant, and fundamentalist Islam. This is understandable since it is these strands in the Islamic world that are involved in conflict and the mass media thrives on covering conflict. However, it is not a level playing field. Instead of isolating political, economic, and military reasons for actions, the mass media portrays all events involving Muslims as religiously motivated behaviour. Violence perpetrated in the name of religion, in Israel, India, the United States, or Sri Lanka, for example, is rarely if ever associated with adherents of that religion. One hardly ever reads about Hindu, Buddhist, Jewish, and Christian terrorists in the world. In the context of violence perpetrated in the United States, Steven Salaita, asks in the context of Nidal Hasan's recent (9 November 2009) massacre of 13 US military personnel,

Quickly. What is Dylan Klebold's religion? Eric Rudolph's? Theodore Kaczynski's? Seung-Hui Cho's? Klebold, you may recall, is one of the two Columbine shooters [in Colorado, United States], Rudolph the Atlanta Olympics bomber [in Georgia, United States], Kaczynski the Unabomber [in Montana, United States], and Cho the perpetrator of the Virginia Tech massacre [in Virginia, United States]. You likely don't know what religion each killer practiced (or, in the case of Kaczynski, practices) because even at the height of their media coverage reporters and commentators didn't tell. It never seemed that important. What is Nidal Hasan's religion? This is the sort of question on which high test scores are made. Unlike his peers in the peculiar American community of disgruntled gunmen, Hasan's religion seems monumentally important. It no more explains his atrocious deed than the (unknown) religions of the other shooters explain theirs, but it does inform an extant belief in the United States that Islam is a rigid progenitor of violence. Any violent action undertaken by somebody identified as Muslim, then, becomes the responsibility of the religion and its 1.3 billion [probably closer to 1.57 billion] followers.

To make matters worse, Islam is perceived as a global threat to Western civilisation and its values. Medieval descriptions of Islam, for example, the 'religion of the sword', the Prophet as a violent person, and Islam as an inherently violent religion, are being recycled into contemporary mass media discourse. Islam is portrayed as a code of belief and action that is irrational, anti-modern, and rigid. This is the so-called 'clash of civilisations' discussed above. One would think that the amount of reliable information written on the Islamic world and the ease of meeting Muslims in the West in the twentieth and twenty-first centuries would have dispelled such ignorance (it has to a certain extent). But it is difficult for a non-specialist to differentiate reliable information about Islam/Muslims from the flood of misinformation that has been published since 2001 in the West. Islamophobia has become a chronic disease, one reinforced by the mass media, religious groups, and other interest groups who benefit, directly or indirectly, from the propagation of fear. . . .

Islam: The Religion of the Sword?

To reiterate, the notion of Islam as the 'religion of the sword' appears to be deeply embedded both in Christendom's and the modern West's collective cultural unconscious. One might suspect that this is due to concrete historical events, for example, in 1453 when Turkish Muslims conquered Constantinople, the centre of Eastern Christendom for over a millennium. From 1529 onward, the 'sword of Islam' turned westward toward Europe as the Ottomans articulated explicit military designs to conquer Europe until the failed Siege of Vienna in 1683. For several centuries, Muslims were a real threat to Christendom and an actual military enemy for 154 years. From a European perspective, Islam was 'the religion of the sword'. These historical events, however, cannot explain the twenty-first century Western fixation of labelling Islam as the 'religion of the sword'. Otherwise, one would expect many other religions to be associated with the sword because all politically influential religions have resorted to violence. Yet Muslims and Jews do not label Christianity as the 'religion of the sword' any more than those conquered by the Tibetans during their period of empire (c. 610–840) labelled Tibetan Buddhism as the 'religion of the sword'. There is thus much more going on.

Objectification of evil [occurs] when an individual unconsciously transfers what he considers negative . . . onto another person or group.

There are data to strongly suggest that Christendom projected its own 'use of the sword' upon the established Muslim 'Other'. Western Christendom stridently labels Islam as the 'religion of the sword' at the time of the Crusades in the Middle East (1095–1291). Sigebert of Gembloux (d. 1112), for instance, starkly contrasts Islam and Christianity. Islam is the religion of the sword while Christianity is the religion of love. He is followed by the influential Peter the Venerable (d. 1156) who also describes Islam as the religion of the sword. Finally, Vincent de Beauvais (d. 1264), the writer of the definitive medieval European encyclopaedia *Speculum Maius*, depicts Muhammad as someone who "converted people to his faith 'with the sword, force and destruction' [...] and Islam as a religion of the sword and vice". These accounts are a sample of Christendom's projections of violence as the Christians themselves are taking up the sword against Muslims. This is only the beginning of Christendom projecting its violent dark side on its chosen external 'Other'. Christendom's involvement in violence demonstrates how powerful the psycho-cultural mechanism of projection can be. . . .

Violence and the 'Dark Side of the West'

It is tempting to think that the modern disease of islamophobia, a fear of Islam and Muslims with no rational basis, is the culmination of centuries of Western European antagonism toward Muslims/Islam. However, it is quite problematic to extrapolate or posit a cause and effect relationship between medieval Christendom's attitudes toward Islam and modern islamophobic discourse and behaviour, even if the language and imagery have remarkable similarities. The question still remains: why is one primary marker for creating the 'Muslim Other' focused on violence? I would argue that Christendom/ the West has been projecting its own violent 'dark side' onto Islam/the Muslims.

This principle of projection in individuals was one of Sigmund Freud's contributions to modern psychology. He postulated that individuals project their own unacknowledged negative character traits on others. The aggregate of these negative traits has been called the 'dark side' because these traits are invisible to the individual. This is how an '(evil) other' is created psychologically. The same principle of projection applies to groups, whether they are tribes, religions, or nations. That is, they project their 'dark side' on other groups, effectively creating an 'other' or an 'enemy'. There is an objectification of evil when an individual unconsciously transfers what he considers negative (and is a part of the individual he chooses not to acknowledge) onto another person or group. "We use them [the other or enemy] for the externalisation of our bad self and object images; these we may superimpose upon (or condense with) the projections of our unacceptable thoughts." A Cypriot Turkish psychologist [Vamik Volkan] discusses his experience:

> In Cyprus, a Greek child learns from what his mother says and does that the neighborhood church is a good place; he unconsciously invests in it for safekeeping his unintegrated good aspects, and feels comfortable being in or near this building. The same mechanism makes him shun the Turkish mosque and minaret, into which he deposits the unintegrated bad aspects of himself [. . .].

Let's investigate very briefly Christendom's involvement in religiously motivated war (which is never only just religious). The Crusades against the Muslims in the Middle East were only one of the many crusades organised by the Popes of the Western Christian church. In the Fourth Crusade (1202–04), Venetian and other Western soldiers attacked fellow Christians and sacked Constantinople. There was the Albigensian Crusade (1209–1229) for 20 years against the Cathars in southern France, as well as the Crusades in the Baltic regions. Estimates of the deaths involved in these last two crusades spiral into the hundreds of thousands. Then there was the Spanish Inquisition (1478–1834), originally set up to convert Spanish Jews and Muslims to Christianity, with an estimated 250,000 deaths involved. In the Christian conquest of the Americas millions of native peoples perished. In passing, one should note how the spread of Islamic rule in the seventh and eighth centuries is called the 'Islamic Conquests', but in the West we never hear about the corresponding 'Christian Conquests' of Eastern Europe, America, Australia, or New Zealand. Even with the lowest population estimate of 10 million inhabitants in the Americas, there were roughly half that number in less than a hundred years after the conquests (1600) and half of that remaining number was exterminated in the ensuing three centuries. According to James B. Wood, the French Wars of Religion (1562–98) had 1,259,220 deaths in just the first 20 years. The bloodiest European war before the nineteenth century was the Thirty Years' War (1618–48) between Protestants and Catholics, which had over 2 million deaths and where an estimated 15 per cent to 20 per cent, if not more, of the population of Germany died.

When we look at the history of pre-nineteenth-century Christendom, we find a very high level of wholesale violence expressed through conquest and deaths from religiously motivated wars. It is true that Christendom was not unique in violence or religiously motivated violence. However, the crucial point is the incongruence between a high level of violence, a self image of Christianity being the 'religion of love', and then the move to define Islam as the 'religion of the sword'. This demonstrates clear denial and projection.

The psycho-cultural factor of projection, or using another group as a 'target of externalisation', is one way of highlighting culturally shared interpretations, which in this study are antagonistic attitudes toward Islam/Muslims. Like Volkan, this article asserts that investigating the process of creating targets of externalisation is useful in explaining the persistence of violence. Islamophobia is a form of violence, especially when one group's own denied violence is projected on to the Muslim Other. I have explained how Christendom's antagonism towards Islam/Muslims developed into one predominant (among others) historically shared social interpretation of Islam. This projected antipathy toward Islam is the cultural legacy in which islamophobia has developed in the West. Unfortunately an association of Islam/Muslims with violence is not only found in the West, but has spread like a virus to other parts of the world via the mass media.

> *There are those . . . who prefer not to acknowledge that such a pathological phobia like islamophobia has deep cultural roots in Christendom/the West.*

This process of 'essentialising the Other' and transferring negative traits is not a monopoly of the West. The governments of many majority-Muslim countries continue to portray the West as 'immoral' and 'decadent', highlighting morally shocking news events in government-controlled media. Egyptian media in the early 1980s, for instance, reinforced this image by televising an American soap opera, "Dallas," which portrayed behaviour that most Americans themselves would also consider morally reprehensible. Labelling the United States as the 'Big Satan' (in Persian; kishwar-i shaytan-i buzurg) by Iranian revolutionaries is another well-known example. Many governments of Muslim countries continue to blame their own homemade present problems on events that happened generations ago rather than taking responsibility for these social and economic problems. Most of this is psychological transference on to former European colonial powers, but in the Arab world this can even involve blaming the Ottoman Turks for present-day problems.

Islamophobia Has Deep Cultural Roots

Using Islam and the Muslims as the West's target of externalisation says much about deep-seated cultural fears in the West. This writer has approached islamophobia as a 'disease', if not a 'virulent disease', that has been fostered by many political, economic, cultural, and religious factors. It is a psychological manifestation of the West's long history of denying its own violence projected upon Islam and Muslims.

There are those, like Fred Halliday, who prefer not to acknowledge that such a pathological phobia like islamophobia has deep cultural roots in Christendom/the West, and prefer an interpretation that "offers more hope" so that then "it is more likely that something can be done". His intent, as I read it, is that one should not essentialise cultural characteristics or people. In this I am in total agreement, since essentialising is a dehumanising concomitant symptom of islamophobia which prevents any possibility of change.

- If the West were inherently anti-Islamic and Islam/ Muslims were inherently violent then a never-ending conflict would be inevitable. This is one of the false assumptions of [political scientist Samuel] Huntington's so-called 'clash of civilisations'. People and cultures have changed, are changing, and will continue to change. Indeed, change is one characteristic that does not change.

- I differ with Halliday, however, on one crucial point. When dealing with a serious disease, not to recognise the chronic condition is to forever be dealing with symptoms. When one suppresses (read denies) symptoms, the chronic condition is only exacerbated. This chronic condition is the denial of violence and the resulting pathological phobia against Islam/Muslims. I personally wish this were not the case, but that is how the disease profile looks.

- We humans have a monumental healing task ahead of us and are seriously challenged to exercise the requisite spiritual skills for this healing process to occur in a timely manner. As many aspects of modern life have become globalised, there is also a simultaneous inter-connectedness of religio-cultural ideas, wisdom, and prejudices.

• Up to this point, the interconnectedness of the preju-dices and the ignorance thereof has overshadowed that of wisdom. Islamophobia is a prime example. Wisdom affirms and nurtures our common human reality of being one family. Increasingly closer contact between differing cultures, ideas, and ways of living is not being matched by increased awareness of who we are. This creates conditions such that misunderstandings and prejudices surface much more easily, are denied, and in turn projected on to growing minorities.

• There is thus a need to balance a heart-felt acknowl-edgement of our common humanity with the acknowl-edgement of the factors preventing this greater aware-ness, e.g., our 'dark side'.

Global warming and environmental degradation are well publicised, but what about the increasing fear of 'the Other' around the world? If we cannot live with each other as we come increasingly in closer contact, then the resultant social strain will be at least as dangerous as these other global prob-lems.

The United States, an immigrant society, is having difficul-ties with the scale of population shifts, primarily involving the mushrooming population of Hispanics and the increasingly public use of Spanish. In Europe it is the Muslim communi-ties that are the focus of paranoia. Despite millions of immi-grants, the nations of Europe are not immigrant countries and they do not have a historical record of multiculturalism. The increasing multicultural reality in large cities of the world, along with large movements of people as refugees and immi-grants, is another factor to consider. This is all potential fuel for increasing islamophobia. Combine this with economic uncertainty and the use of fear by governments to control their populations, and it is a formula for targeting minorities and immigrant communities. Denial, projection, and the lack of self-awareness are psycho-spiritual luxuries that we can no longer afford. We human beings either chart a common destiny or there will be no earthly destiny for anyone.

In closing, there is thus no room for mutual distrust—that is to say, for undifferentiated hatred for the West/Westerners from the part of Muslims on the one hand and 'islamophobia' from the part of the West/Westerners on the other.

A Small Group of Right-Wing Zealots Is Responsible for Spreading Islamophobia

Wajahat Ali et al.

Wajahat Ali is a researcher and writer at the Center for American Progress.

On July 22, [2011] a man planted a bomb in an Oslo [Norway] government building that killed eight people. A few hours after the explosion, he shot and killed 68 people, mostly teenagers, at a Labor Party youth camp on Norway's Utoya Island.

The 2011 Oslo Bombing Was Incited by Anti-Muslim Propaganda

By midday, pundits were speculating as to who had perpetrated the greatest massacre in Norwegian history since World War II. Numerous mainstream media outlets, including *The New York Times*, *The Washington Post*, and *The Atlantic*, speculated about an Al Qaeda connection and a "jihadist" [holy war] motivation behind the attacks. But by the next morning it was clear that the attacker was a 32-year-old, white, blond-haired and blue-eyed Norwegian named Anders Breivik. He was not a Muslim, but rather a self-described Christian conservative.

According to his attorney, Breivik claimed responsibility for his self-described "gruesome but necessary" actions. On July 26, Breivik told the court that violence was "necessary" to save Europe from Marxism and "Muslimization." In his 1,500-

page manifesto, which meticulously details his attack methods and aims to inspire others to extremist violence, Breivik vows "brutal and breathtaking operations which will result in casualties" to fight the alleged "ongoing Islamic Colonization of Europe."

Breivik's manifesto contains numerous footnotes and in-text citations to American bloggers and pundits, quoting them as experts on Islam's "war against the West." This small group of anti-Muslim organizations and individuals in our nation is obscure to most Americans but wields great influence in shaping the national and international political debate. Their names are heralded within communities that are actively organizing against Islam and targeting Muslims in the United States.

Breivik, for example, cited Robert Spencer, [an] anti-Muslim misinformation [scholar] ..., and his blog, Jihad Watch, 162 times in his manifesto. Spencer's website, which "tracks the attempts of radical Islam to subvert Western culture," boasts another member of this Islamophobia network in America, David Horowitz, on his Freedom Center website. Pamela Geller, Spencer's frequent collaborator, and her blog, Atlas Shrugs, was mentioned 12 times.

Geller and Spencer co-founded the organization Stop Is-lamization of America, a group whose actions and rhetoric the Anti-Defamation League concluded "promotes a conspiratorial anti-Muslim agenda under the guise of fighting radical Islam. The group seeks to rouse public fears by consistently vilifying the Islamic faith and asserting the existence of an Islamic conspiracy to destroy 'American values.'" Based on Breivik's sheer number of citations and references to the writings of these individuals, it is clear that he read and relied on the hateful, anti-Muslim ideology of a number of men and women detailed in this report—a select handful of scholars and activists who work together to create and promote misinformation about Muslims.

While these bloggers and pundits were not responsible for Breivik's deadly attacks, their writings on Islam and multiculturalism appear to have helped create a world view, held by this lone Norwegian gunman, that sees Islam as at war with the West and the West needing to be defended. According to former CIA [US Central Intelligence Agency] officer and terrorism consultant Marc Sageman, just as religious extremism "is the infrastructure from which Al Qaeda emerged," the writings of these anti-Muslim misinformation experts are "the infrastructure from which Breivik emerged." Sageman adds that their rhetoric "is not cost-free."

A small group of foundations and wealthy donors are the lifeblood of the Islamophobia network in America.

A Small Group Spreads Hate and Fear of Muslims

These pundits and bloggers, however, are not the only members of the Islamophobia infrastructure. Breivik's manifesto also cites think tanks, such as the Center for Security Policy [CSP], the Middle East Forum, and the Investigative Project on Terrorism. . . . Together, this core group of deeply intertwined individuals and organizations manufacture and exaggerate threats of "creeping Sharia [Islamic law]," Islamic domination of the West, and purported obligatory calls to violence against all non-Muslims by the Koran.

This network of hate is not a new presence in the United States. Indeed, its ability to organize, coordinate, and disseminate its ideology through grassroots organizations increased dramatically over the past 10 years [between 2001 and 2011]. Furthermore, its ability to influence politicians' talking points and wedge issues for the upcoming 2012 elections has mainstreamed what was once considered fringe, extremist rhetoric.

And it all starts with the money flowing from a select group of foundations. A small group of foundations and wealthy donors are the lifeblood of the Islamophobia network in America, providing critical funding to a clutch of right-wing think tanks that peddle hate and fear of Muslims and Islam—in the form of books, reports, websites, blogs, and carefully crafted talking points that anti-Islam grassroots organizations and some right-wing religious groups use as propaganda for their constituency.

Some of these foundations and wealthy donors also provide direct funding to anti-Islam grassroots groups. According to our extensive analysis, here are the top seven contributors to promoting Islamophobia in our country:

- Donors Capital Fund

- Richard Mellon Scaife foundations

- Lynde and Harry Bradley Foundation

- Newton D. & Rochelle F. Becker foundations and charitable trust

- Russell Berrie Foundation

- Anchorage Charitable Fund and William Rosenwald Family Fund

- Fairbrook Foundation

Altogether, these seven charitable groups provided $42.6 million to Islamophobia think tanks between 2001 and 2009 . . .

And what does this money fund? Well, here's one of many cases in point: Last July [2011], former Speaker of the House of Representatives Newt Gingrich warned a conservative audience at the American Enterprise Institute that the Islamic practice of Sharia was "a mortal threat to the survival of freedom in the United States and in the world as we know it."

Gingrich went on to claim that "Sharia in its natural form has principles and punishments totally abhorrent to the Western world."

Sharia, or Muslim religious code, includes practices such as charitable giving, prayer, and honoring one's parents— precepts virtually identical to those of Christianity and Judaism. But Gingrich and other conservatives promote alarmist notions about a nearly 1,500-year-old religion for a variety of sinister political, financial, and ideological motives. In his remarks that day, Gingrich mimicked the language of conservative analyst Andrew McCarthy, who co-wrote a report calling Sharia "the preeminent totalitarian threat of our time." Such similarities in language are no accident. Look no further than the organization that released McCarthy's anti-Sharia report: the aforementioned Center for Security Policy, which is a central hub of the anti-Muslim network and an active promoter of anti-Sharia messaging and anti-Muslim rhetoric.

American Muslims and Islam are the latest chapter in a long American struggle against scapegoating based on religion, race, or creed.

In fact, CSP is a key source for right-wing politicians, pundits, and grassroots organizations, providing them with a steady stream of reports mischaracterizing Islam and warnings about the dangers of Islam and American Muslims. Operating under the leadership of Frank Gaffney, the organization is funded by a small number of foundations and donors with a deep understanding of how to influence U.S. politics by promoting highly alarming threats to our national security. CSP is joined by other anti-Muslim organizations in this lucrative business, such as Stop Islamization of America and the Society of Americans for National Existence. Many of the leaders of these organizations are well-schooled in the art of getting attention in the press, particularly Fox News, *The Washington Times*, and a variety of right-wing websites and radio outlets.

Misinformation experts such as Gaffney consult and work with such right-wing grassroots organizations as ACT! for America and the Eagle Forum, as well as religious right groups such as the Faith and Freedom Coalition and American Family Association, to spread their message. Speaking at their conferences, writing on their websites, and appearing on their radio shows, these experts rail against Islam and cast suspicion on American Muslims. Much of their propaganda gets churned into fundraising appeals by grassroots and religious right groups. The money they raise then enters the political process and helps fund ads supporting politicians who echo alarmist warnings and sponsor anti-Muslim attacks.

These efforts recall some of the darkest episodes in American history, in which religious, ethnic, and racial minorities were discriminated against and persecuted. From Catholics, Mormons, Japanese Americans, European immigrants, Jews, and African Americans, the story of America is one of struggle to achieve in practice our founding ideals. Unfortunately, American Muslims and Islam are the latest chapter in a long American struggle against scapegoating based on religion, race, or creed.

Around the world, there are people killing people in the name of Islam, with which most Muslims disagree.

Due in part to the relentless efforts of this small group of individuals and organizations, Islam is now the most negatively viewed religion in America. Only 37 percent of Americans have a favorable opinion of Islam: the lowest favorability rating since 2001, according to a 2010 ABC News/*Washington Post* poll. According to a 2010 *Time* magazine poll, 28 percent of voters do not believe Muslims should be eligible to sit on the U.S. Supreme Court, and nearly one-third of the country thinks followers of Islam should be barred from running for president.

Alienating Muslims Is Counterproductive

The terrorist attacks on 9/11 [2001] alone did not drive Americans' perceptions of Muslims and Islam. President George W. Bush reflected the general opinion of the American public at the time when he went to great lengths to make clear that Islam and Muslims are not the enemy. Speaking to a roundtable of Arab and Muslim American leaders at the Afghanistan embassy in 2002, for example, President Bush said, "All Americans must recognize that the face of terror is not the true faith—face of Islam. Islam is a faith that brings comfort to a billion people around the world. It's a faith that has made brothers and sisters of every race. It's a faith based upon love, not hate."

Unfortunately, President Bush's words were soon eclipsed by an organized escalation of hateful statements about Muslims and Islam from the members of the Islamophobia network. . . . This is as sad as it is dangerous. It is enormously important to understand that alienating the Muslim American community not only threatens our fundamental promise of religious freedom, it also hurts our efforts to combat terrorism. Since 9/11, the Muslim American community has helped security and law enforcement officials prevent more than 40 percent of Al Qaeda terrorist plots threatening America. The largest single source of initial information to authorities about the few Muslim American plots has come from the Muslim American community.

Around the world, there are people killing people in the name of Islam, with which most Muslims disagree. Indeed, in most cases of radicalized neighbors, family members, or friends, the Muslim American community is as baffled, disturbed, and surprised by their appearance as the general public. Treating Muslim American citizens and neighbors as part of the problem, rather than part of the solution, is not only offensive to America's core values, it is utterly ineffective in combating terrorism and violent extremism.

The White House recently [August 2011] released the national strategy for combating violent extremism, "Empowering Local Partners to Prevent Violent Extremism in the United States." One of the top focal points of the effort is to "counter al-Qa'ida's propaganda that the United States is somehow at war with Islam." Yet orchestrated efforts by the individuals and organizations detailed in this report make it easy for al-Qa'ida to assert that America hates Muslims and that Muslims around the world are persecuted for the simple crime of being Muslims and practicing their religion.

America Has a History of Witch Hunts

Sadly, the current isolation of American Muslims echoes past witch hunts in our history—from the divisive [Senator Joseph] McCarthyite purges of the 1950s to the sometimes violent anti-immigrant campaigns in the 19th and 20th centuries. New York Mayor Michael Bloomberg has compared the fearmongering of Muslims with anti-Catholic sentiment of the past. In response to the fabricated "Ground Zero mosque" controversy in New York last summer, Mayor Bloomberg said:

> In the 1700s, even as religious freedom took hold in America, Catholics in New York were effectively prohibited from practicing their religion, and priests could be arrested. Largely as a result, the first Catholic parish in New York City was not established until the 1780s, St. Peter's on Barclay Street, which still stands just one block north of the World Trade Center site, and one block south of the proposed mosque and community center.... We would betray our values and play into our enemies' hands if we were to treat Muslims differently than anyone else.

[A] word about the term "Islamophobia." We don't use this term lightly. We define it as an exaggerated fear, hatred, and hostility toward Islam and Muslims that is perpetuated by negative stereotypes resulting in bias, discrimination, and the marginalization and exclusion of Muslims from America's social, political, and civic life.

It is our view that in order to safeguard our national security and uphold America's core values, we must return to a fact-based civil discourse regarding the challenges we face as a nation and world. This discourse must be frank and honest, but also consistent with American values of religious liberty, equal justice under the law, and respect for pluralism. A first step toward the goal of honest, civil discourse is to expose—and marginalize—the influence of the individuals and groups who make up the Islamophobia network in America by actively working to divide Americans against one another through misinformation.

Islamophobia Grew Following 9/11

Goal Auzeen Saedi

Goal Auzeen Saedi is a contributor to the Millennial Media blog at the Psychology Today website.

It seems almost un-American to say it. The tragedies of 9/11 [2001] had grave ramifications for countless individuals ranging from the victims' families, crisis response teams including the NYPD and NYFD [New York Police Department and New York Fire Department], and the nation at large. But there was also another population that suffered deeply that many fail to mention. They are Arab and Muslim Americans.

In the U.S., there are roughly 5.4 million Muslims made up of African Americans, South Asians, and Arabs; additionally, there are approximately 2.5 million non-Muslim Arabs residing in the U.S. Hence, the events following 9/11 marked a significant turning point for many minority groups. Discrimination and hate crimes rose sharply, and in the nine weeks following September 11th, the Arab Anti-Discrimination Committee confirmed over 700 violent acts against Arabs and on those perceived to be Arab. The FBI [Federal Bureau of Investigation] reported a 1600% increase in hate crimes against this group in the year following 9/11.

In many European countries, discriminatory acts often were perpetrated against those who visibly looked Muslim such as Hindus and Sikhs. The accidental shooting of a Brazilian man by British police who looked Muslim after the London bombing attacks attests to this very finding. It appears that religious affiliation is a greater determinant of such discrimination as opposed to ethnicity, or other cultural markers. Thus, appearance as a Muslim, regardless of actual religious affiliation is a major predictor of hate crime and other forms of discrimination. Such discriminatory attitudes lay the foundation for the intensification of Islamophobia that occurred after 9/11.

What Is Islamophobia?

The term "Islamophobia" was first coined in 1922 by Etienne Dinet, a French Orientalist painter who throughout his career became interested in Arabic culture and Islam. However, the term came into common usage in 1997 as a result of the British Runnymede Trust Commission on British Muslims. They define the term as "dread or hatred of Islam and therefore, to the fear and dislike of all Muslims." The term is similar to xenophobia and has become part of our common usage particularly following the events of 9/11.

While Islamophobia has been problematic . . . [for] many Muslims, its toxic nature has spread to the public domain as well through the media.

Perhaps the most comprehensive study of Islamophobia following 9/11 was conducted by the European Monitoring Center on Racism and Xenophobia, which examined Islamophobic sentiment and discrimination across 15 European nations. Their findings suggest that although violent abuse was relatively low (though not to say nonexistent), there were higher reports of harassment, aggression, and verbal abuse.

In viewing the widespread nature of post 9/11 Islamophobia, it has been posited that perhaps pre-existing Islamophobic sentiment was reawakened after the terrorist attacks, suggesting this form of discrimination has existed in many nations prior to 9/11. Through examining pre and post 9/11 discriminatory attitudes, it was found that indirect discrimination rose by 82.6%, and overt discrimination rose by 76.3%, while 35.6% of study participants suffered mental health problems as a result of this.

Muslims and Islamophobia in the Media

While Islamophobia has been problematic in the private lives of many Muslims, its toxic nature has spread to the public domain as well through the media. It is quite evident that the Western media has and continues to negatively portray Muslims and Arabs in both the news media and film. According to [Narmeen El-Farra in an article titled "Arabs and the Media"], many newspapers make liberal use of terms such as fanatics and extremists, in addition to terrorists to describe individuals from the Middle East. In 1995 when the Oklahoma City bombings occurred, many early reports suggested it was the work of Muslim terrorists, thereby reinforcing the notion of Muslims as anti-American criminals.

In addition to the explicit discriminatory attitudes being expressed freely about Muslims in the news media, there has been much concern regarding a similar phenomenon in film. [Jack G.] Shaheen has extensively studied stereotypes pertaining to Arabs in film, and in one film analysis ["Reel Bad Arabs: How Hollywood Vilifies a People"] found over 50 films that vilify Arabs as the enemy. He describes how in numerous films, "Arabs are brute murderers, sleazy rapists, religious fanatics, oil-rich dimwits, and abusers of women."

He traces the creation of this stereotype which has been reinforced repeatedly for over 40 years through film. Among his conclusions regarding the perpetuation of this stereotype include the fact that "bash-the-Arab movies make money," and public silence. This includes silence from audiences, as well as Arabs, none of whom figure prominently in the film industry, whether as producers or celebrities. Shaheen reports that American film producers and directors often point to the news to justify their portrayals, stating, "We're not stereotyping . . . just look at your television set. Those are real Arabs."

How Muslims Are Perceived as Dangerous

The portrayal of Muslims as dangerous has in fact affected the psyche of the nation. The "shooter bias" paradigm is well-known in discrimination research, indicating that when asked to respond quickly to threatening situations, individuals are more likely to become aggressive toward minority rather than Caucasian perpetrators of violence. While much of this research has examined the bias toward shooting at Black versus White targets in simulation video games, most recently, research has indicated a "turban effect." Here, individuals donning cultural or religious garb such as a turban or *hijab* [traditional head covering for Muslim women] are shot in these studies more frequently than those without, suggesting this shooter bias to be the result of internalized negative stereotypes toward these minority groups.

Muslim Women Wearing Traditional Head Coverings Face Prejudice

Additionally, implicit negative attitudes toward Muslims are not limited to the idea of dangerous terrorist men. A series of studies focusing on the hijab have provided surprising insights about the perception of Islamic head coverings worn by some women. For example, one study used photographs of Caucasian and South Asian women both with and without hijab, and found that when covered, these women were rated significantly less physically attractive and intelligent than when these same individuals did not wear this attire.

Another study found women who wore hijab often had lower expectations of obtaining employment, with expectations being lowered as a function of public contact associated with the job, and higher job status. The findings of this study suggest a manifestation and realization of stereotype threat, as reports indicated as much as a 153% increase in workplace discrimination claims against Muslims following 9/11.

Hence, while 9/11 was a serious loss for the nation at large, and we come to commemorate the 10th anniversary of this great tragedy, we find there are many reasons to mourn. For as the nation struggled to make sense of the nonsensical and inhumane, another group simultaneously found itself lost as it grieved as Americans as well as Muslims. The generation of young Muslims that grew up during 9/11 had the misfortune of being raised during the time of the "war on terror." They heard taunts of being called "Osama" and "ragheads."

The Economic Crisis Has Contributed to Islamophobia

Rachel Slajda

Rachel Slajda is a reporter at Portfolio Media.

Nine years after Sept. 11, 2001, America saw perhaps its worst outbreak of Islamophobia since the attacks. Experts wagered it came from the aimless fear and the anger people feel in times of economic crisis, exploited by certain politicians looking to give their party an advantage in the midterms and turned toward American Muslims. Such an outbreak was possible in the days and months after Sept. 11's attacks. It never really materialized, experts say, in part because President George W. Bush stood up and told the nervous country that Islam is a religion of peace, and that American was not at war with Muslims.

He made no such appeal this year, and President [Barack] Obama's pleas fell on deaf ears or, more accurately, ears that believe Obama himself is secretly, and sinisterly, Muslim. Without further ado, then, is This Year [2010] in Islamophobia:

The 'Ground Zero Mosque'

When an imam [prayer leader of a mosque]—a known moderate imam who'd been sent by the U.S. government around the world on goodwill missions to Muslim nations—and a group of developers decided to turn the old Burlington Coat Factory building in downtown Manhattan into a community center and mosque, almost no one noticed. No one noticed for months, in fact, until all of a sudden, this summer, it exploded. People like Pamela Gellar and Robert Spencer, who for years had been screaming about the dangers of Islam from the fringe, were suddenly front and center. Their assertions—that American Muslims are inherently dangerous, that the majority of imams are radical, that Imam Feisal Abdul Rauf is a terrorist sympathizer—were suddenly being repeated by the mainstream, by Newt Gingrich, Sarah Palin and the like.

When . . . Terry Jones announced that he would burn . . . Korans . . . on Sept. 11, the media dug in and didn't let go.

People said vicious things, calling the community center a shrine to terrorists and salt in an American wound.

The furor came to a head on Sept. 11, the ninth anniversary of the attacks, when protesters from both sides converged on the site, just a few blocks from Ground Zero itself and the memorial services being held. They screamed and chanted, and at least one man tore pages out of the Koran and scattered them throughout the street. Then, as suddenly as it came, the furor died down to a few embers at the extremes. But the community center is still years and millions of dollars away from being a reality, and we can all expect more outrage to come.

The Koran Burner

When cultish Florida church leader Terry Jones announced that he would burn a pile of Korans in his front yard on Sept. 11, the media dug in and didn't let go. It became the biggest story of the week, with dozens of reporters and news crews camped out in front of Jones' church, while reporting that footage and even stories about such a bonfire could set off violent riots in the Muslim world and give recruiting fodder to terrorists.

So worried was the Obama administration that Defense Secretary Robert Gates called Jones personally to ask him not to burn any Korans. He eventually agreed to call off the event after a local imam told him that Rauf, the New York imam, had promised to move his community center, even though he hadn't. Jones never did go through with it.

The spectacle angered the "God hates fags" funeral protesters at the Westboro Baptist Church, who'd been burning Korans for years.

It also prompted copycats, like the man in Texas who tried to burn one of the holy books but was thwarted by a skateboarder, who described the incident thusly: I snuck up behind him and took his Koran, he said something about burning the Koran, I said, "Dude you have no Koran," and ran off.

Sharia in Middle Tennessee

The opposition to a mosque near Murfreesboro, Tenn., started out scary—first with vandalism and then with an arson that claimed some of the mosque's construction equipment. But it quickly turned to farce, as opponents to the Islamic Center of Murfreesboro—which has been in town for 30 years and is now trying to expand—filed a lawsuit to try and stop it.

The lawyers for the opponents, partially funded by a Christian Zionist group [a Christian group supporting Jewish sovereignty in Israel], argued in county court that the mosque's permit for religious use should never have been approved because Islam, they claimed, isn't a religion. When the Justice Department filed a brief noting that the U.S. has recognized Islam since Thomas Jefferson's time, the lawyers claimed that the federal government couldn't be trusted because it had once condoned slavery.

The judge ruled that the mosque's construction could continue.

The Future

Violence has, fortunately, not spread past isolated incidents like the young man who slashed a Muslim cab driver in New York City.

But the story of Islamophobia in America is not over. Tensions between the Muslim community and federal law enforcement are growing, as the FBI [Federal Bureau of Investigation] continues to conduct undercover terror stings that some critics say amounts to entrapment. The new chairman of the House Homeland Security Committee, Rep. Peter King (R-NY) has claimed that Muslim leaders are insufficiently cooperative with terror investigations and therefore is holding hearings on the "radicalization" of Muslim Americans. Other congressmen have promised to try to keep the hearings from targeting Muslims. And so what happens next year, and the year after that—whether cooler heads continue to prevail in the end—remains to be seen.

The Perceived Oppression of Muslim Women Is Used to Justify Islamophobia

Leila Ahmed

Leila Ahmed is an Egyptian-American writer on Islam and Islamic feminism and the first women's studies professor at Harvard Divinity School.

For those of us who have worked in the field of women in Islam for years the changes which overtook our field after 9/11 [2001] were dramatic and profound. Just on the most facile level for example, the topic went from being one that a few of us feminists and academics were interested in, to being one about which heads of state and world leaders—most recently for example France's president [Nicolas] Sarkozy, were apt to have strong opinions about. From being something we studied in libraries it became a topic we now followed in the media—where, under one guise or another, it often now figured on the front pages or in the headlines.

Interest in Women and Islam Grew After 9/11

In particular of course the hijab [traditional head covering for Muslim women]—in any of its forms—burqah [enveloping outer garment for Muslim women] hijab, niqab [face veil worn by Muslim women]—would now periodically erupt as an issue of state in western nations. Previously hijabs had, of course, been matters of state in some Muslim majority countries—Saudi Arabia and Iran for example, where hijab was required by law, and Turkey and Egypt both of which had recently banned it from schools and other venues. But here it was now, in the post-9/11 era, beginning with France's ban on the headscarf in schools in 2004, becoming a matter of national import to the West too.

The burka became the "battle flag" and "shorthand moral justification" for the war in Afghanistan.

It was shortly after 9/11 and as we went to war in Afghanistan that the subject of women and Islam first erupted into public political discourse in America and the West. It would be articulated at the highest level of the Administration on November 17, 2001 when First Lady Laura Bush gave a radio address in which she spoke of women's oppression in Afghanistan as a matter of national import.

"Civilized people throughout the world," she said, "are speaking out in horror—not only because our hearts break for the women and children of Afghanistan, but also because in Afghanistan we see the world the terrorists would like to impose on the rest of us. The fight against terrorism is also a fight for the rights and dignity of women."

The Burka as Shorthand Moral Justification for War

Two days later Cherie Blair, wife of then British Prime Minister Tony Blair, issued a similar statement. Taking their cue from the first ladies, the media now portrayed the war in Afghanistan as a righteous war by virtue of our concern to save the women.

As a British journalist wrote at the time, the burka became the "battle flag" and "shorthand moral justification" for the war in Afghanistan. In the ensuing months the media filled with images of burka, images embedded in narratives that were about women's oppression in Afghanistan, but narratives too that often also carried an implicit message as to Islam's purportedly ageless oppression of women.

Of course, invoking the theme of the oppression of women in Islam as justification for war and domination is nothing new to the history of western imperialism. In fact this rhetoric of "saving the women" in the name of "civilization" is an old ploy used many times in the past in particular by British and French imperialists.

This was rhetoric they used with regard to women in whatever regions their empires took them to—in relation to Muslims or Hindus or others—to justify imperial domination. It was about precisely this rhetoric that [Indian-American scholar] Gayatri Spivak, back in the 1980s, coined the now famous phrase, of "white men saving brown women from brown men."

Astoundingly, to those of us familiar with this history, here it was again this old ploy, resuscitated, dusted off, and being replayed all over again—and, even more astonishingly it was actually working. It was entirely commonplace now to hear that we were in Afghanistan to save the women from the atrocities of the Taliban [militant political group in Afghanistan]—which as I said, was implicitly understood too to be those innately of Islam.

For, as of 9/11, the subject of women in Islam typically figured in our political discourse almost always to evoke the meaning of "the oppression of women in Islam".

And in turn, the theme of the oppression of women in Islam itself is almost always a code for fear, suspicion, dislike of Islam: and consequently it is code therefore also for justifying policies targeting Muslims and/or mobilizing consent in support of wars in Muslim majority countries.

Mobilizing Feelings of Hostility

It is of course extremely important to bear in mind that it is in this particular decade that the subject of women in Islam has suddenly soared to prominence in the political discourses of western nations. This obviously has been an eventful and turbulent decade in the history of Islam and the West.

Inaugurated by an act of violence committed in the name of Islam against America—and followed by wars in Afghanistan and Iraq, two Muslim majority countries, to the accompaniment throughout of new tensions constantly arising in western societies around issues of Muslim immigrants and their descendants, these surely have been unprecedented times in modern history as regards relations between Islam and the West—and certainly in any case as regards American relations with Muslims and the Muslim-majority world.

Such is the political and social context and environment in which this subject has now gained prominence and come to be evoked to serve what are often essentially political goals. . . .

As such scholars and critics point out, it's an arresting fact that books by Muslim women recounting their personal oppressions under Islam soared in popularity in the very years that our wars in Iraq and Afghanistan were in fact costing many mostly Muslim women their very lives.

Remarkably, they point out, in the period in which the general public was apparently—judging by these best-selling books—deeply empathizing with Muslim women oppressed by Islam, they were simultaneously apparently not much disturbed, let alone outraged, at the unnumbered lives of Muslim women and children destroyed in these wars.

So reviewing this history and the troubling political uses which the subject of the oppression of women in Islam is serving today, my overall conclusion then is that it is time now really that we deleted this entire subject of "the oppression of women in Islam" from our repertoire. It's a subject that is, in reality, no more than a rhetorical device without meaning or content, a device that we've inherited from imperial times. It's time to cast it aside.

It would be obviously absurd if anyone were to write or speak today about the oppression of women in Christianity—by which they sweepingly meant whatever injustices and opressions Christian women were suffering in, say, Nigeria, India, Argentina, Russia and Italy.

Yet this is routinely how the oppression of women in Islam is typically evoked today in popular discourse. Wheras in fact the injustices and oppressions Muslim women suffer vary enormously depending on where they live: those suffered by women living in Saudi Arabia, Iran, Indonesia, Turkey, France, and the U.S.A. vary enormously and it would be nearly meaningless to lump them all together.

Direct Confrontation of Unjust and Cruel Laws

In saying that its time to set aside the old imperial rhetoric of the oppression of women in Islam, I am certainly not arguing, I should make clear, that I believe that particular interpretations of Islam do not include attitudes and laws that are indeed appallingly unjust to women. On the contrary I believe that there are all too many such examples.

But the way forward is not through the wholesale denigration of "everything Islamic or through grand assaults on the oppression of women" in Islam, but rather through directly confronting and challenging unjust and cruel laws, customs and behaviours one by one and specifically, wherever they occur.

Banning Face Veils
Fuels Islamophobia

Nancy Graham Holm

Nancy Graham Holm is a journalist.

Out of a total Muslim population between four and six million, the French government estimates no more than 2,000 women wear a *burqa/niqab* [full face veil or full body garment]. Nevertheless, full face veiling in public has been illegal in France since April [2011] and those who violate the law risk a €150 fine. Those who support the law say they are worried about veiled women compromising the nation's secular foundations and undermining women's dignity that comes with gender equality. In addition, some claim that Muslim men are forcing these women to cover their faces, resulting in oppressive isolation. On the other side, opponents argue the law is a pretext to reduce the visibility of Muslims in public spaces.

A Challenge to France's Full Face Veil Ban

What then should we think about the political campaign of Kenza Drider, a 32-year-old mother of four who wears *niqab?* By running for public office, she is asserting her right to speak in public and participate in democracy, exercising the very civil rights that many westerners claim Muslims do not value. Although she won't be declared an official candidate until she gets the signature of 500 elected officials, Madame Kenza is serious about her campaign, which she sees as a platform from which to challenge [French president] Nicolas Sarkozy's ban on full face veiling. "I tried to understand this law," says Drider, the long shot Presidential candidate from Avignon, "and what I understood is that this is a law which puts us under house arrest."

All traditional depictions of the Virgin Mary show her veiled and nuns have copied this for centuries.

It's hard to see this Muslim woman as oppressed. Maybe Kenza Drider and her colleagues are misguided but they are hardly crushed and isolated. Muslim women are intelligent and need to be left alone to find their own way. "When I was very young I wore the hijab [head scarf] and after one year I knew it wasn't right for me," says Egyptian journalist, Mona Eltahawy, "but I wore it for nine years and I say it took me eight years to take it off." It is not the government's business to tell women how to dress, says British Muslim journalist and women's rights activist, Shelina Zahra Janmohamed.

The issue is modesty, but modern scholars agree the particular verses in the Qur'an (24:31–32) asking for it are exceedingly vague and ambiguous. *"Believing women should lower their gaze and guard their modesty; they should not display their zeenah (charms, beauty or ornaments) except what must ordinarily appear thereof; they should draw their outer garments over their bosoms."* The ambiguity is so significant, says religion historian Reza Aslan, "that a woman who reads the scripture and says 'I am absolutely certain that I am supposed to veil' is just as right as the woman who reads the same scripture and says 'I am absolutely certain that I do not have to veil.'" According to Muslim legal philosopher, Abdullahi Ahmed An-Na'im of Emory University, only 30–40% of the world's Muslim women cover their heads or faces either as a deliberate sign of piety or as a political statement.

Education Is the Answer, Not Government Intervention

Historians are also quick to remind us that covering the head has been a concept in Judaism and Christianity as well as in Islam. All traditional depictions of the Virgin Mary show her veiled and nuns have copied this for centuries. Until the 1960s, women who entered Roman Catholic churches were required to cover their hair. Contemporary Orthodox Jewish men still wear the small yarmulke as a sign of respect to God and Jewish law requires married women to cover their hair. Kenza Drider inherited—or perhaps adopted—an interpretation of verses 24:31–32 that is ultra conservative. Whether she'll ever choose another interpretation or not, she should have the right to dress as she wants.

In the meantime, there are Muslims who hope to change the hearts and minds of their ultra conservative colleagues through education and debate, not government intervention. Taj Hargey at MECO (Muslim Education Center of Oxford) heads a campaign against full face veiling because he calls it masking and says it has nothing to do with Islam. "It is a pre Islamic custom from Byzantium and Persia that was later integrated into Muslim society and then given a veneer of religion as justification." Shelina Zahra Janmohamed wears a headscarf but she, too is opposed to full face veiling because she interprets the phrase: "except what must ordinarily appear" as a woman's face. "I also believe that Islam is strong on opinion and personality," she says "and I feel that making sure the face is uncovered allows people to express who they are and assert some kind of identity."

"What the French law has done," says Drider, "is give citizens the right to insult veiled women." This means that full face veiled women seen on the street, on public transportation, shopping or picking up their children from school are fair game for ridicule and contempt. And since there are already moves to create similar legislation in Belgium, The

Netherlands and Italy, this means the law is contributing to Islamophobia. Surely, this is counter-productive when what we need are public policies and personal practices that bridge gaps instead of creating them. Let's hope that the courageous Kenza Drider and her campaign will bring these issues into public debate.

CHAPTER 2

Is America Islamophobic?

Chapter Preface

The August 30, 2010, *Time* magazine cover story was "Islamophobia: Does America Have a Muslim Problem?" Prompted by the controversy over the plans to build a Muslim cultural center and mosque two blocks from Ground Zero in Manhattan and opposition to the building of mosques in other parts of the country, the article examined whether or not these controversies were symptomatic of a growing intolerance of Muslims in America. The article concluded that, while "Islamophobia in the US doesn't approach levels seen in other countries where Muslims are a minority," still, "where ordinary Americans meet Islam, there is evidence that suspicion and hostility are growing." A *Time* poll finding that 46 percent of Americans believed Islam was more likely than other faiths to encourage violence against nonbelievers was cited in support of a growing unease with the Muslim faith in America.

This position was rebutted by Jeff Jacoby in an Op-Ed piece in the *Boston Globe* on December 8, 2010. "America is many things, but 'Islamophobic' plainly isn't one of them. As *Time* itself acknowledged: 'Polls have shown that most Muslims feel safer and freer in the US than anywhere else in the Western world,'" Jacoby argued. To support his contention, the author cited Federal Bureau of Investigation (FBI) statistics on hate crimes in the United States showing that just 9.3 percent of all hate crimes motivated by religious bias were committed against Muslims—significantly fewer than the 70.1 percent committed against Jews.

A report titled "Islamophobia and Its Impact in the United States: January 2009–December 2010," sponsored by the Council on American-Islamic Relations (CAIR) and the University of California at Berkeley's Center for Race and Gender, concluded:

"America is not an Islamophobic nation, but it has Islamophobic elements:

- The public's favorable rating of Islam sank from 40 percent in November 2001 to 30 percent in August 2010 according to the Pew Research Center.

- In late Novemeber 2010, the Public Research Institute found that 45 percent of Americans agree that Islam is at odds with American values.

- A *Time* magazine poll released in August 2010 found, 'Twenty-eight percent of voters do not believe Muslims should be eligible to sit on the US Supreme Court. Nearly one-third of the country thinks adherents of Islam should be barred from running for President.'"

While surveys may report an increasing distrust of Muslims in America, this finding isn't shared by Muslim-Americans. A comprehensive public opinion survey conducted in August 2011 by the Pew Research Center of 1,033 Muslims living in America revealed that while many believe that life for Muslim-Americans in post-September 11, 2001, America is difficult in a number of ways, they perceive no significant changes in discrimination or harassment since a similar poll conducted in 2007.

The differing views in these surveys, reports, and commentary are emblematic of the controversial nature of the charge that America is an Islamophobic nation. In the following chapter, commentators and journalists debate whether or not America is Islamophobic.

Anti-Muslim Sentiment Is Widespread in the United States

Peter Beinart

Peter Beinart is senior political writer for the Daily Beast and an associate professor of journalism and political science at City University of New York. He is also a senior fellow at the New America Foundation and the author of The Crisis of Zionism.

How would the American right have responded had Anders Behring Breivik been a Muslim? Luckily, we don't have to guess. In the immediate aftermath of Friday's [July 20, 2011] terrorist attack in Norway, conservative *Washington Post* blogger Jennifer Rubin did us the favor of simply assuming that he was a Muslim. She then used the attack to denounce lawmakers who in the name of deficit reduction favor "huge cuts in defense" and to lambast President [Barack] Obama for suggesting "that we can wrap up things in Afghanistan."

Anti-Muslim Bigotry Is Widespread in the United States

But had Breivik actually been a Muslim, I suspect Rubin's efforts to tie the attack to the Afghan war and the defense budget would have quickly been overtaken by the search for his American counterparts: homegrown Muslim terrorists. Conservative commentators would have ridiculed liberals for opposing [US representative] Peter King's recent hearings into American Muslim radicalization. They would have demanded that law-enforcement officials cease their politically correct pussyfooting and begin racially profiling Muslims (or dark-skinned people who look like Muslims). Some even would have suggested that Norway had been naive to admit so many Muslims into the country and urged that we not make the same mistake. The media's primary question in the wake of the Breivik attack would have been, Can it happen here? And conservatives would have answered, Hell yes.

Terrorism usually stems from the intersection between militant ideology and mentally vulnerable people.

So let's ask that question about the real Breivik attack: Could an anti-Muslim bigot commit a large-scale terrorist attack in the U.S.? The answer is, Absolutely, because the same anti-Muslim bigotry that influenced Breivik in Europe is widespread here.

Much Recent U.S. Terrorism Has Been Right-Wing

There's actually been a lot of right-wing, extremist Christian terrorism in the U.S. in recent years. The biggest terrorist attack in U.S. history prior to 9/11—the 1996 Oklahoma City bombing—was carried out by Timothy McVeigh, a white ex-Army officer with ties to the militia movement. That same year, Eric Rudolph bombed the Atlanta [Georgia] Olympics to protest abortion and international socialism. The only major WMD [weapons of mass destruction] attack of the "war on terror" era—the 2001 anthrax mailings—apparently was the handiwork of a microbiologist angry that prominent Catholic politicians were pro-choice. In 2009, anti-abortion militants murdered Wichita doctor George Tiller. (He already had been shot once, and his clinic had been bombed.) That same year octogenarian neo-Nazi, James Wenneker von Brunn, shot a security guard at the U.S. Holocaust Memorial Museum. Last February [2010], Andrew Joseph Stack, angry at the federal government, flew a small plane into an IRS [Internal Revenue Service] building in Austin, Texas.

Islamophobia Is an Obsession of the Right Wing

The attacks on Muslims have been smaller in scale. Last August, during the "Ground Zero" mosque controversy, a Manhattan man stabbed a cabdriver after asking if he was a Muslim. The following month witnessed an arson attack against the site on which a mosque was being built in Tennessee. This May [2011], the words "Osama today, Islam tomorrow" were spray-painted on a mosque in Maine. But what makes a larger, Breivik-style attack possible is that terrorism usually stems from the intersection between militant ideology and mentally vulnerable people. That's why people like McVeigh and Rudolph latched onto extremist militia and anti-abortion ideology in the 1990s. And it's why their equivalent today might well be influenced by Islamophobia, the current obsession of America's extreme right.

Islamophobia is at least as prevalent on the political right today as militia-style, anti-government conspiracy-theorizing was in the 1990s. Herman Cain, who according to a June [2011] *Des Moines Register* survey is running third in Iowa and who in February won the Tea Party convention's straw poll, has said he would not appoint a Muslim to his cabinet or as a federal judge. He's opposed the building of the Tennessee mosque whose construction site was the subject of last year's arson attack. And he has said he became "uncomfortable" when he learned that the surgeon who operated on his liver was Muslim. More than a dozen states, mostly in the reddest parts of the south and mountain west, are considering banning Sharia [Islamic law]. Tim Pawlenty recently shut down a Minnesota program that helped observant Muslims buy homes without violating Islam's prohibition on collecting or paying interest on loans. And Newt Gingrich has warned that by the time his grandchildren grow up, America may be "dominated by radical Islamists."

Some conservatives have condemned some of this. Even Rubin recently said that Herman Cain "lacks an understanding of the Constitution. And he certainly isn't ready to be president." But the criticism doesn't remotely approximate the outrage that would have followed similar statements about Jews, Christians, African-Americans, or almost anyone else. It's painfully clear that in today's Republican Party, the price of publicly opposing anti-Muslim bigotry is higher than the price of fueling it. And somewhere out there, someone like Anders Behring Breivik is watching.

Islamophobia Has Replaced Anti-Semitism in the United States

Nadine Epstein

Nadine Epstein is editor and publisher of Moment *magazine.*

M uslims have replaced Jews as targets of discrimination.

During the 1940s and 1950s, some Jewish scientists were stripped of their security clearances, causing them to lose their jobs or be downgraded to lower-security projects. One of the most famous cases was that of physicist J. Robert Oppenheimer, known as the "father of the atom bomb," who lost his clearance in 1954 because he had belonged to a group that also included communist members. "I think it is desirable that the U.S. population, especially its younger members, be reminded of that historical hysteria," says Edward Gurjuoy, emeritus professor of physics at University of Pittsburgh and a former chair of the American Physical Society Committee on the International Freedom of Scientists.

Today, Muslims are more likely than Jews to lose security clearances, says Sheldon Cohen, a security clearance lawyer in northern Virginia. "I am finding discrimination against Muslims because of their religion and because of Islamophobia," he says, adding that he finds no evidence of anti-Semitism today.

Muslims Are Losing Their Security Clearances

Muslims employed by the federal government who have lost clearance include Egyptian-born Dr. Moniem El-Ganayni. A nuclear physicist naturalized as an American citizen, his security clearance was revoked in 2007 by the Department of Energy. The American Civil Liberties Union (ACLU) took El-Ganayni's case to U.S. District Court after the government—contrary to its own policy—denied the scientist the chance to contest the revocation and refused to divulge the reasons behind it, citing "national security."

Although such cases are difficult to win in court . . . the clearance suspension process has significantly improved since the 1950s.

El-Ganayni lost his appeal for a hearing and, as a result, his job at the Bettis Atomic Power Lab in West Mifflin, outside Pittsburgh, Pennsylvania. "After September 11," says El-Ganayni's attorney Witold Walczak, legal director of the Pennsylvania ACLU, "there was a hyper-vigilance about Muslims and as a result you have some law-abiding Muslims who are unfairly targeted and punished simply because they are Muslim."

Another high profile case concerned Wagih Makky, also an Egyptian-American. According to court documents, the Federal Aviation Administration (FAA) hired Makky, a technical expert in aviation security, to create a special anti-terrorism unit for passenger jets after the 1988 bombing of Pan Am Flight 103. After 13 years developing technology to detect and prevent explosives from detonating aboard commercial planes and passenger trains—first for the FAA, then for the Transportation Safety Administration—Makky's clearance was revoked, leading to his dismissal. ACLU also failed in its efforts to challenge this in the justice system.

Although such cases are difficult to win in court—judges are loath to second-guess the government on security clearance issues—the clearance suspension process has significantly improved since the 1950s, says Steven Aftergood, director of the Project on Secrecy for the Federation of American Scientists. "Executive Order 12968 issued under the [Bill] Clinton Administration in 1995 established more clarity as well as new procedures for seeking reconsideration of adverse decisions," he says. "The concept of the whole person" means that while "you may have been a convicted criminal in the past, that doesn't guarantee that you cannot hold clearance in the future. At the same time the playing field is not level. It is the government that decides who will or will not receive a clearance." You can appeal but you are only guaranteed an explanation.

Americans with Muslim Names Have a Harder Time Finding a Job

According to the Equal Employment Opportunity Commission, American Muslims have experienced increased job discrimination since 2001. Complaints alleging anti-Muslim bias in the workplace numbered nearly 800 for the year ending September 30, 2010, up about 20 percent from 2008 and showing a nearly 60 percent spike from 2005. In fact, Muslims account for just over 21 percent of religious discrimination cases despite comprising less than one percent of the population.

While discrimination on the basis of religion was outlawed by the 1964 Civil Rights Act, a 2004 study by the non-profit Discrimination Research Center shows that Muslim names have become a liability for job-seekers. Six thousand similar, fictitious resumes were sent to California employment firms with names "identifiable" as white, Latino, African American, Asian American and Arab American. The name Heidi McKenzie received the highest positive response rate, 36.7 percent, and Abdul-Aziz Mansour, the lowest, 23 percent.

According to Biplab Pal, a Bangladeshi-American engineer who has served as a hiring manager for American engineering firms, it has become tougher for educated minorities, including Muslims and Indian and Bangladeshi Hindus who look like Muslims, to obtain white-collar jobs in the U.S. "Many minority engineers are changing their names to American-sounding Christian names to get a job," says Pal.

Islamophobia Has Replaced the Fear of Communism

Since September 11, the balance between security issues and civil liberties in the United States has tilted toward security and fighting terrorism. "Muslim terrorist" has replaced "communist" and echoes of [anti-Communist former senator Joseph] McCarthy can be heard. Popular conservative websites such as WorldNetDaily and scholars such as M. Stanton Evans, author of *Blacklisted by History: The Untold Story of Senator Joe McCarthy and His Fight Against America's Enemies*, argue that McCarthy was on the right track and that liberals, who once hindered the struggle against communists, now hinder the fight against terrorism.

On the flip side are those who believe that the government is using methods comparable to those used in the 1940s and 1950s. Its "modus operandi" [mode of operation] was to create lists of proscribed organizations, then investigate, prosecute and fire individuals based on their affiliations with these proscribed groups," says David D. Cole, a constitutional law professor at Georgetown University Law School. "It has been revived in the post-9/11 era. The suspect associations have changed. People don't care if you get the Communist Party Worker's magazine but they would care if you get the Hamas newspaper."

The equation of Islam with terrorism troubles Akbar Ahmed, professor of Islamic Studies at American University in Washington, DC. "Unless we become aware of the problem and look at historical comparisons with the Jewish community 50 years ago, the stereotypes won't go away," he says. He points to the congressional hearings that are underway to "investigate radical Islam." "It's a good idea to talk about these issues, but I am concerned it will become a media circus," he says. "That's what happened to the Jewish community half a century ago."

Bigots Are Responsible for the Spread of Islamophobia to Mainstream Americans

Mosharraf Zaidi

Mosharraf Zaidi has served as an advisor on international aid to Pakistan for the United Nations and European Union and writes a weekly column for Pakistan's The News.

One of the lessons from the Quran-burning circus in Florida [after the announcement by Terry Jones that he would burn copies of the Quran on the anniversary of 9/11], whether it ever actually takes place or not, is that the labels we use to make sense of the world are becoming more and more complex. This is bad news. Labels are supposed to simplify life, not make it more complicated. Nine years to the day since al Qaeda attacked New York City, murdered nearly 3,000 people, and changed the world we live in, our labels seem to be leading us down some strange paths.

Narrow-Minded Bigots Are Spreading Islamophobia

In Pakistan, "Talibanization" is a label used to describe regressive and parochial conservatism, not just the political ascendancy of Mullah Omar and his extremist disciples. When we use the label "mullah," it is not the same thing as honoring someone by calling him "Father" or "Reverend." Instead, we're most likely referring to a person's narrow-mindedness, bigotry, and possible racism. So when we try to explain to fellow Pakistanis how the United States is much grander than the pettiness of Quran-burning circuses or mosque-defying ex-

Mosharraf Zaidi, "The Talibanization of America," *Foreign Policy*, September 10, 2010.

tremists, we don't use the same labels that Americans would. Describing the ideological kith and kin of opponents of the Park51 [the Islamic Cultural Center planned to be built near Ground Zero] project—including the fringe element of folks like Terry Jones and his flock at the Dove World Outreach Center—with terms like the moral majority, far-right evangelicals, or even neocons is useless.

An Islamophobia problem in America is a problem everywhere else.

Instead, when we try to explain what is happening in America, we simply say that a great country is going through a kind of Talibanization—led by mullahs like Newt Gingrich, Pamela Geller, and the occasional Terry Jones.

On the ninth anniversary of the atrocities of September 11, 2001, applying these labels to right-of-center America may seem provocative and harsh. After all, even the most grotesque Islamophobia in the United States is not guilty of the horrors enacted by the Taliban, in Afghanistan and beyond. More than any other sin, the Taliban tolerated Osama bin Laden, defended his right to stay among them, and refused to hand him over after he boastfully acknowledged his role as the chairman and CEO of al Qaeda's war on America.

But consider the alternative: What if we didn't present the Quran-burners and mosque-attackers as part of a fringe movement of ideologically driven extremists? Then of course, the only other possibility is for us to accept that International Quran Burning Day and the controversy over the Park51 community center both in different ways signify mainstream America's growing discomfort with Islam. Simply put, if the Islamophobia of an American fringe is in fact not on the fringes, but in the mainstream, then the United States has an Islamophobia problem.

The United States Is Unpopular in Muslim Countries

And an Islamophobia problem in America is a problem everywhere else. Of all the things that can destroy the fragile and momentous little steps of progress across the Muslim world, this might be the most potent and lethal. In some of the world's most important Muslim majority countries, already, America is deeply unpopular. A Pew Global Attitudes survey this year [2010] revealed that the four countries with the deepest anti-American sentiment are Egypt, Jordan, Turkey, and Pakistan. Three of these receive busloads of U.S. taxpayer cash, as aid. The fourth, Turkey, is the only modern nation-state from among almost 60 Muslim-majority countries in the world.

State Department do-gooders in Washington and around the world may wonder whether the United States can afford any further ill will in these countries. But the real problem is that the already fraught balance between Islam and the rest of the world can't afford the kind of bitterness and hatred that an Islamophobic America—real or imagined—would unleash. Muslims with feet in both worlds often try to bridge the distance between these worlds by invoking the freedom and vitality of Islam in America. The specter of an irrational Islamophobia in America would gut that argument.

Until recently, growing up Muslim in America was arguably one of the most uniquely Islamic experiences in the world. Muslims in the United States enjoy the ironclad protections of the First Amendment, the overwhelming, if often grudging support of the liberal establishment, and at the microlevel (between individuals and families) common cause with their Christian and Jewish cousins of the Abrahamic faith tradition. For the most part, unless you happened to be a Muslim African-American, Muslims had it good in America.

That explains, at least partially, why the most progressive and robust religious voices in global Islam aren't coming from

Pakistan, or India, or Indonesia, or the Arab world. Instead, they are coming from places like California's Zaytuna Institute, and from a certain New York community leader named Feisal Abdul Rauf.

Progressive thought is being lost in the places where it would matter the most.

In the places where the 9/11 attacks were planned, financed, and conceived, meanwhile, the warm and fuzzy Islam of America's suburbs is a nonexistent fantasy. On the Muslim Main Street, in Saudi Arabia, in Afghanistan, and in flood-ravaged Pakistan, Muslims can't see past the Talibanized narrative of the U.S. mid-term election. Just as the mainstream news media in America cannot be held responsible for transforming Terry Jones from a walking punch line into an international celebrity, mainstream media in a country like Pakistan can hardly be blamed for reporting Jones's shenanigans to 180 million—mostly Muslim—Pakistanis.

On Sept. 10 [2010], as Afghans celebrated Eid, many decided to protest against the Islamophobic events planned in Florida. During the protests, NATO [North Atlantic Treaty Organization] troops, surrounded by angry protesters, opened fire, killing at least one person in Badakhshan province. It is easy to become partisan in assigning blame for this death. Many will blame Terry Jones. Others will blame the media. Many others will blame the mullahs who stoked Afghan anger. No doubt, some pundit at Fox News will blame the protester himself, and most people in Afghanistan will blame NATO.

It barely matters anymore who pulled the trigger in Badakhshan. The point is that progressive thought is being lost in the places where it would matter the most. In the nine years since 9/11, there has not been a single domestic Muslim reawakening in any of the Organization of the Islamic Conference's almost 60 Muslim-majority countries. In countries like Pakistan, mosque leaders still make the same anti-American references. They still exhibit the same resistance to change. They still get treated with kid gloves by governments that are run by culturally dislocated Muslims.

Mainstream Americans Are Susceptible to Fear Tactics

Stuck between the growing contempt for traditional Muslim values in the American mainstream, and the regressive inertia of traditional Muslim societies around the world, are the real victims of bin Laden's perverted violence, as well as the disproportionate and self-defeating military responses that now have the seal of approval of two successive U.S. presidents.

The most dubious aspect of the industrious coverage of burning Qurans and protests against the building of a Muslim community center of course, is that on this ninth anniversary, justice and closure seem as far away for the victims of 9/11 as they did nine years ago. The hundreds of thousands of dead Iraqis and Afghans have brought little, if any comfort to the 9/11 families.

Drone attacks in Pakistan may offer some, but only as long as the faces and names of the innocent victims of those drones remain shrouded in mystery. Conversely, all the rage and anti-Americanism can't seem to liberate countries like Pakistan and Egypt from their corrupt, self-serving, and vicious elite. Instead, vitriolic protests and U.S. flag burning ceremonies help keep those elite firmly ensconced in power—as they milk the emotions of their people with one hand, and the ever-ready teat of U.S. military and civilian assistance with the other.

In the United States, decent people are unleashing unkind and hateful words upon Muslims around the world because they can. Their rage has nothing to do with Islam. It has everything to do with living in a country that is up to its eyeballs in debt and cannot seem to generate new jobs or new ideas, even under a president who was supposed to lift their country out of this morass.

There Are Hopeful Signs

Still, all hope is not lost, in America, or around the Muslim world. Mikey Weinstein's Military Religious Freedom Foundation promises to donate one Quran to the Afghan National Army for every Quran burned by Terry Jones' congregation.

The American Jewish tradition of defending civil liberties has been reawakened, with numerous Jewish groups rallying to the defense of Islam in America. Among them are the Religious Action Center of Reform Judaism, the National Council of Jewish Women, and a host of others. They are all acting in concert with various Christian denominations to support the Interfaith Coalition on Mosques—which has pledged to act as a watchdog on Islamophobia when it comes to mosque building in the United States.

Terry Jones's own home state of Florida has offered a poignant reminder of America's multifaith tradition. Larry Reimer, a minister at the United Church of Gainesville, has decided, "If they can burn it, then we can read it." On Sept. 12 [2010], his congregation will include, as part of its Sunday worship, a reading from the Quran.

Perhaps the most brilliant ray of light in this darkness comes from a Facebook group to which I was invited this week [of September 10, 2010]. A number of young Pakistanis set up "BLESS the Bible Day on September 11." As I'm writing this, the group already has 150 members—more than three times the number that Pastor Terry Jones cons into listening to him every Sunday.

There is much to be worried about on this ninth anniversary of 9/11. It is hard, however, to worry too much in the face of the mercy and love of people of all faiths reaching out to each other to fight the hatred and bitterness. Had that spirit prevailed across the mainstream media in the United States, perhaps we'd have a lot less to talk about this 9/11—focusing instead on the tremendous strength of the innocent families that lost loved ones on that day.

Anti-Muslim Sentiment Is a Problem on College Campuses

Akbar Ahmed and Lawrence Rosen

Akbar Ahmed is the Ibn Khaldun Chair of Islamic Studies at American University in Washington, DC; Lawrence Rosen is the William Nelson Cromwell Professor of Anthropology at Princeton University and adjunct professor of law at Columbia University.

With the dramatic opening last month [March 2011] of the U.S. House of Representatives' Homeland Security Committee hearing on "the extent of radicalization in the American Muslim community," the country was once again confronted with anti-Muslim sentiment based on fear. The recent dispute over the building of an Islamic community center near Ground Zero, legislative proposals in 15 states to bar consideration of Islamic law in American courts, and the founder of Tea Party Nation calling for a Muslim-free Congress are a few examples of why the United States must carefully examine its relationship with the approximately seven million Muslims who live here, and the nearly one out of four individuals on the planet who subscribe to Islam.

Islamophobia Is Encroaching onto U.S. Campuses

College and university campuses are not immune to the wave of Islamophobia. Consider Geert Wilders's 2009 speech at Columbia University in which he stated that "the Koran is an evil book, full of violence, murder, terrorism, war," and that "Muhammad was not a perfect man—he was a mass murderer and a pedophile," or the public outcry and polarizing lectures last fall when Brooklyn College assigned Moustafa Bayoumi's book *How Does It Feel to Be a Problem? Being Young and Arab in America* to entering students as part of its Common Reader program.

Fear of Muslims has been exacerbated by professors in the booming field of terrorism and security studies, who not infrequently characterize Islam as an inherently violent religion. Those who speak favorably of Islam come under fire from organizations like Campus Watch, which monitors what professors are saying and applies its substantial resources to challenging the reputations of those with whom it disagrees. This has created an ugly atmosphere on some campuses, as professors teaching courses on Islam may have to worry about how their remarks might be reported and how that may affect their careers.

If combating ignorance is the overarching mission of educators, then not since the great era of civil-rights awareness in the 1960s has there been such a compelling need for involvement by the academic community on behalf of a minority population. Unfortunately, today such involvement is neither widespread nor growing. Yet it is critical that educators formulate appropriate and imaginative responses, in their classrooms and on their campuses, to this anti-Muslim culture. While no single solution fits all circumstances, certain possibilities are worth consideration.

For instance, when potentially divisive lectures are contemplated, two formats might be entertained: a debate or a jointly sponsored talk. The former has the benefit of a stylized yet civil form of discourse; the latter would involve both sides of contentious issues, thus promoting an atmosphere of civility engendered by the interest of each in having its viewpoint granted serious consideration. Indeed, using planning meetings of student organizations not only to co-sponsor and mediate presentations but to contribute to an exchange of viewpoints leading up to the lecture or debate may help establish shared standards of procedure.

Such joint involvement may not, of course, be sufficient to avoid all disruptions. When such disturbances do occur, however, the participants should be subject to university disciplinary proceedings—to the standards of which each presenting organization should be required to subscribe.

The Study of Islam Should Be More Inclusive

One of the most effective ways to achieve greater understanding is to have students in a variety of courses make contact with members of the local Muslim community and enter into discussions with them. Social-science students could include interviews with people in the area or arrange and analyze a community meeting; literature students could organize a reading by Muslim poets or writers; art students could discuss with local congregations the way in which an American mosque is being designed. Such field-based projects, organized as part of coursework, can help produce useful ethnographic information as well as provide opportunities for meaningful local interaction.

The stakes of the debate about Islam could not be higher.

To counter pervasive stereotypes, we need solid sociological accounts that will address the development of homegrown terrorists, the generational conflict within many Muslim families, and the roles played by Muslim religious leaders and the boards that run their mosques—studies the academy has so far failed to provide. Faculty can also make themselves available to local groups for lectures. The extensive experience of the authors at such events clearly suggests that one is not merely preaching to the converted: Local church and synagogue groups often simply do not know how to contact Muslims in their area. Universities can act as facilitators in such cases.

Universities also must take a close look at their own programs, including "terrorism studies" classes, and ask themselves if those courses are conveying an accurate view of Islam and the Muslim world. This can be done through faculty forums on teaching, so that no one professor feels under scrutiny, and all can be encouraged to build into their courses some component that discusses, in a realistic and accurate way, the nature of Muslim life, science, art, and politics.

It may not, of course, be possible to compel civility. But we do know that when groups have a vested interest in gaining access to a campus forum, the opportunity presents itself to develop shared rules of the road. One can always go too far in this regard: The British experience with its Anti-Social Behaviour Order, aimed at punishing disruptive or discourteous acts, has demonstrated that civility is not advanced when standards are overly broad or purely subjective. But the recent creation of the University of Arizona's National Institute for Civil Discourse, whose honorary chairs are Presidents George H.W. Bush and Bill Clinton, suggests that universities may serve our society as a base for imagining alternative ways of carrying on our conversations.

The stakes of the debate about Islam could not be higher. Just as it was the academy that so effectively combated claims of scientific racism and has so assiduously fought against stereotypes of women as less capable or academically talented than men, so, too, the image of Islam and of Muslim cultures must be wrested from those who have dominated the terms of discussion in ways that are both misleading and dangerous.

"Knowledge" is the second-most frequently used word in the Koran, after the name of God. And there is no university whose mission fails to give the pursuit of understanding equally high priority. At a time when Muslims are acting in consort with our own revolution—courageously rising up against tyrants and laying down their lives to resurrect their dignity and authenticity—the academy owes them and our fellow Muslim citizens every effort to think creatively about this people and this faith. This we must do if, in years to come, we are to answer the question, "Where were you then?" with all the energy and pride that our universities' pursuit of truth requires of us.

Anti-Muslim Bigotry Is Exaggerated

Russ Smith

Russ Smith is a publisher and columnist who founded the Baltimore City Paper, Washington City Paper, New York Press, *and the website Splice Today.*

How many roads must a man walk down before he realizes the ghost of Joseph McCarthy is not lurking around every corner? It's a pertinent question today [September 15, 2010], in the midst of a tumultuous Congressional midterm election campaign, as aghast and pissed off liberals are pointing fingers aimlessly looking for someone to blame. You'd think that pundits—elite or scruffy, left- or right-wing—might finally understand that constantly evoking [Adolf] Hitler, [Joseph] Stalin, Mao [Tse-Tung] and [Joseph] McCarthy in propping up this or that argument, just has no credibility anymore. Barack Obama's not a socialist or undocumented alien, just as George Bush didn't have a shrine to the Third Reich in a cubbyhole at the White House.

Comparisons to the McCarthy Era Are Exaggerated

Peter Beinart, one of the most pretentious of the early middle-aged Beltway/New York intelligentsia, hasn't received that message, as his latest *Daily Beast* post, "The New McCarthyism" amply demonstrates. It's Beinart's contention that America is in "the midst a national psychosis: the worst spasm of paranoia and bigotry of the post-Cold War age." Had he been referring to the appalling anti-immigrant fervor directed mostly at Mexicans and other Hispanics, I could see his point, if not the hyperbole. But no, in the wake of the ongoing debate about the plans for an Islamic center near Ground Zero in Lower Manhattan (which will probably never come to fruition) and a publicity-seeking minister from Florida who threatened to burn a copy of the Koran, Beinart insists "the American Muslim" is the symbol for everything U.S. citizens fear.

This is predictable and far too easy: yes, loudmouths like Sarah Palin and Newt Gingrich (whom Beinart cites) are quick with a slur against Muslims to audiences they consider appropriate and advantageous to their own political goals. But if Beinart's going to raise the Joseph McCarthy specter, shouldn't he at least provide some evidence of Congressional inquisitions of Muslim-Americans (which haven't occurred under the presidencies of either Bush or Obama), blacklisted men and women in academia, entertainment or even those applying for a mortgage or credit card, or mass deportations borne of rampant Islamophobia? After all, it's not as if the United States has made it a crime for Muslim women to wear a burqa or other full-body robes: no, that was France—France!—the allegedly enlightened European intellectual paradise that Hollywood liberals often threaten to move to if a Republican is elected president.

Ratcheting up the rhetoric, Beinart concludes by playing the Yom Kippur card at the conclusion of his misguided article: "It's an ancient idea, the scapegoat, onto which the nation transfers its burdens and sins. Now we Americans have a new one, the American Muslim, and a new set of sins for which we will, I pray, one day atone." Good gravy! I don't dispute Beinart's opinion that there exists a degree of anti-Muslim bigotry in this country today, but if there's been a rash of torched mosques and murders of devout Muslims I've missed the news reports.

There Was No Backlash of Anti-Muslim Sentiment After the 9/11 Attacks

Jonathan S. Tobin

Jonathan S. Tobin is executive editor of Commentary.

On August 25, 2010, a New York City cabdriver was slashed and stabbed by a drunken passenger who allegedly accompanied his assault with anti-Muslim remarks. The driver, Ahmed H. Sharif, a native of Bangladesh, survived the attack, and the accused assailant was quickly arrested and faces a stiff prison sentence. Attacks on New York cabdrivers are not unheard of, but this incident quickly assumed the nature of a symbol of American intolerance for Muslims because of the contentious national debate over plans to build an Islamic community center two blocks from Ground Zero—the site of the former World Trade Center destroyed in the terrorist attacks of September 11, 2001.

Muslim-Americans Have Been Safeguarded, Not Harassed

Polls consistently showed that the majority of New Yorkers and Americans thought the placing of the planned 13-story Islamic center and mosque on the site of a building that was among those devastated by debris from the 9/11 assault on the towers was, at best, insensitive and, at worst, an affront to the victims. But after months of debate, much of the public discussion about the topic had by the time of the attack on

Jonathan S. Tobin, "The Mosque and the Mythical Backlash: False Fears About Anti-Muslim Bias Have Distorted the Debate Over the Proposal for an Islamic Center Near Ground Zero," *Commentary*, Vol. 130, No. 3, October 2010, p. 24. Copyright © 2010 by Commentary. All rights reserved. Reproduced by permission.

Mr. Sharif come to be centered on a different question altogether: the peril faced by American Muslims.

Indeed, many in America's political and media elite had come to characterize virtually any opposition to the planned Islamic center, no matter how finely nuanced and devoid of prejudice against Islam, as more a product of bigotry than concern about the propriety of such a scheme. In a speech given with the Statue of Liberty as a backdrop, the city's mayor, Michael Bloomberg, proclaimed that nothing less than the principle of religious liberty was at stake. Later he would say that all critics of the so-called Cordoba Initiative (a name that was quickly changed to the more neutral Park51 from one that invoked the era of Muslim rule in Spain) "should be ashamed of themselves" and that any compromise about the site of the project was out of the question, since to oppose the presence of a mosque in the shadow of Ground Zero was a form of bigotry that must be defeated at all costs. The cover of *Time* asked, "Does America Have a Muslim Problem?" The New York cabbie attack was seen as the culmination of weeks of contention that was concrete proof that it does.

How had the debate over this project turned from one about what seemed to many Americans an ill-considered provocation into one about the victimization of Muslims? The answer lies in the formation of a narrative about the aftermath of 9/11 that has sought to establish as fact that a massive backlash against all Muslims took place in the wake of the attacks. This idea, promoted largely by American Islamic and Arab groups whose own bona fides as opponents of terrorism is questionable, holds that a strain of Islamophobia has seized hold of the country in the past nine years. As *Time* put it: "to be a Muslim in America now is to endure slings and arrows against your faith—not just in the schoolyard and the office but also outside your place of worship and in the public square, where some of the country's most powerful mainstream religious and political leaders unthinkingly (or worse, deliberately) conflate Islam with terrorism and savagery." If one were to accept this statement as true, then it was possible to believe that all those who questioned the Ground Zero project, no matter what their avowed motives, were fellow travelers of an invidious movement whose purpose was to delegitimize Islam and to harass its believers.

Americans have been incessantly lectured by their leaders to the effect that Islam is a "religion of peace."

But the problem with this narrative is that it is false. While incidents of anti-Muslim or anti-Arab discrimination or violence have taken place, any attempt to portray such acts as representative of American attitudes toward Muslims is entirely unfounded. It would be far closer to the truth to characterize post-9/11 America—from the statements and policies enacted by its leaders to much of the content of the mainstream media—as having been dedicated to a great degree to *safeguarding* American Muslims from such discrimination.

Despite the searing impact of the 9/11 attacks on the national consciousness, rather than feeding hatred of those identified as having a connection with the enemy, as is historically the case with virtually any country at war, American popular culture has largely avoided the use of Arabs and Muslims as stereotypical villains in films and television shows since 2001. Governmental action against suspected terrorists and those who fund such activities has been narrowly cast: despite the nation's post-9/11 emphasis on security, racial profiling of young Muslim males, which experience shows are the most likely terror suspects, has been banned. Though stories of Muslims being subjected to unfair questioning at airports are legion—guilty only of "flying while Muslim"—security procedures designed to avoid targeting Muslims have made it just as likely for *anyone*, even those who are the least likely to be possible terrorists, to be harassed by security personnel.

Starting with President George W. Bush in the immediate aftermath of the 9/11 attacks, Americans have been incessantly lectured by their leaders to the effect that Islam is a "religion of peace" and that the overwhelming majority of Muslims don't support anti-American terrorism. This has been repeated on both national and local levels after every subsequent instance of Muslim-based terror against Americans. The FBI [Federal Bureau of Investigation] has devoted significant resources to reaching out to Muslims, thereby securing their cooperation in investigations of terrorists and also reassuring them of the government's goodwill and disinclination to view all adherents of Islam as in any way responsible for the actions of terrorists. Indeed, every time such a crime was committed or plot uncovered in the United States, as several were in just the past two years, the reflex of nearly all political, religious, and media figures is first to warn the public against tarring all Muslims with the brush of terrorism before exploring the possibility that some form of Islam might have inspired the crime—if the latter is addressed at all.

There Has Been Minimal Violence Against Muslims

Even more to the point, though largely isolated incidents of anti-Muslim violence such as the New York cabbie attack are deplorable, there is no empirical evidence that there has been anything like a surge of violence against Muslims since 9/11 or that Muslims or Arabs have been singled out for more bias attacks than any other religious or ethnic group. FBI hate-crime statistics compiled in the years since 9/11 flatly contradict the thesis that Muslims have suffered disproportionately from such attacks. In 2000, the FBI recorded 28 instances of anti-Islamic hate crimes. That went up considerably to 554 in 2001, the year of 9/11, but then went down in 2002 to 170. That number remained relatively stable throughout the decade. The total for 2008, the most recent year for which statistics are available, was 105 reported attacks motivated by anti-Islamic bias. Meanwhile, in every year from 2000 to 2008, the number of hate crimes reported against Jews far outnumbered those against Muslims. Even in 2001, when anti-Islamic violence peaked, more than twice as many crimes were motivated by anti-Semitism than those rooted in anti-Muslim sentiment. In 2008, there were 1,013 incidents of anti-Jewish crime, a total that comprised nearly two-thirds of all reported religion-based incidents and more than eight times as many as against Muslims.

The most remarkable aspect of the post 9/11 reaction may well be the general absence of discrimination or violence against Muslims.

Those who purport to represent the interests of American Muslims may dispute these figures as underestimating the number of crimes against their community because of reluctance on the part of minorities to cooperate with authorities and report crimes. But even if one believes that the true figures may be higher, the facts make it clear that there has been no wave of anti-Muslim bias.

The comparison to anti-Jewish hate crimes is also instructive. Though it is difficult to estimate the exact number of Muslims in America, Islamic groups are prone to claim that there are approximately 6 million adherents in the United States, a round number that matches the rough estimate for the number of Jews. But even if the number of American Muslims is smaller than the population of American Jews, how is it possible to claim that the nation is racked by Islamophobic violence when it is generally acknowledged that the far greater instances of anti-Jewish attacks do not justify a conclusion that the United States is boiling over with anti-Semitism?

Indeed, the most remarkable aspect of the post 9/11 reaction may well be the general absence of discrimination or violence against Muslims. Even in the first days after the attacks, when both the American people and its government awakened to the realization that a terror network of Islamists considered itself at war with the United States, the impulse to characterize this fight as a conflict against Islam per se has been consistently rejected.

Though some, such as Imam Feisal Abdul Rauf, the driving force behind the Ground Zero project, have rationalized the attraction of Muslims to anti-American violence by claiming that "the United States has more Muslim blood on its hands than al-Qaeda has on its hands of innocent Muslims," American policy has never strayed from the concept that the war on terror was never one against Islam but against Muslims who had distorted their religion and were, in fact, more likely to target more moderate co-religionists than Americans. Indeed, with more than a billion Muslims and the need for help from Muslim nations and the foes of al-Qaeda and the Taliban in Iraq and Afghanistan, how could America's stance be any different? Despite the desire of some to demonize U.S. military action in the Middle East as a war on Islam, the number of Muslims who have been liberated from oppressive regimes by virtue of the power of the U.S. military is astonishing—more than 45 million in Bosnia, Iraq, and Afghanistan.

Certain Muslim Groups Exaggerate Muslim Oppression

Why then are Muslim groups and their friends in the mainstream media so intent on claiming that Islamophobia is running amok in the land? A leading factor is that the best-known American Muslim organizations were largely founded on this notion that America is a foe of Islam. Perhaps the most prominent such group, the Council on American-Islamic Affairs

(CAIR), was created in the early 1990s as the political and public-relations arm of the Holy Land Foundation, an Islamic charity whose purpose was to raise funds in the United States to benefit the Hamas terrorist organization. Though the Holy Land Foundation was eventually shut down by the Treasury Department and prosecuted in federal court (during the course of which records documenting CAIR's Hamas ties were revealed and it was named an unindicted co-conspirator), CAIR has expanded its reach. It has sprouted chapters around the country; gained access at times to Congress, the Department of Justice, and the White House; and its leaders have become frequent talking heads on television.

The effort to marginalize justified criticism of Islamism has gone hand in hand with the gradual acceptance of the myth of the post-9/11 backlash.

CAIR's political agenda has been dedicated to expressing criticism of the alliance between the United States and Israel while also opposing American efforts to restrain radical Islamic regimes such as Iran. But CAIR has also, in conjunction with other groups, such as the American Muslim Council and the Anti-Arab Discrimination Committee, pursued a parallel agenda of portraying American Muslims as besieged by a tide of prejudice, discrimination, and violence. Its arguments are couched in the sociological jargon of antibias advocacy in large measure because there is, as the FBI hate-crimes statistics show, little except the "anecdotal evidence" cited by *Time* to back up their claims.

In this manner, such groups have entrenched themselves as the voice of American Muslims—even though it is arguable that the majority of this population, composed for the most part of hard-working immigrants, are more interested in gaining a piece of the traditional American dream than rationalizing the behavior of Hamas, Hezbollah, or Iran. By doing so, these groups have promulgated a perspective that seeks to blur the line between radical Islamists and the rest of the Muslim world. From this frame of reference, one that has been increasingly accepted by liberals in the media, any critic of Islamism as well as groups like CAIR may be smeared as an anti-Muslim racist who does not deserve a hearing—a factor that played a significant role in the attempt to bulldoze those questioning the Park51 project.

The effort to marginalize justified criticism of Islamism has gone hand in hand with the gradual acceptance of the myth of the post-9/11 backlash. The success of this campaign about Muslim victimization is made plain by a September 2009 survey conducted by the Pew Forum on Religion and Public Life. This poll found that 58 percent of Americans believed that Muslims are subject to "a lot of discrimination" far more than say the same about Jews, evangelical Christians, or Mormons—despite empirical evidence that says otherwise. With the notion of Muslim victimhood—a prized status in America's contemporary media culture—firmly established, the groundwork was laid for the Ground Zero mosque controversy.

The Park51 Project Became a Political Lightning Rod

The debate about the Park51 project began slowly. Few objections were raised when the property at 45 Park Place, which served as a Burlington Coat Factory store until 9/11, was sold to a real-estate group composed of Muslim investors in July 2009. Since the attack occurred before the store had opened for business, no one was hurt when the landing gear of one of the hijacked planes crashed through the roof and through two empty selling floors of the building. (Project backers who scoff at the notion that the building is part of the Ground Zero area have ignored the fact that the site was itself hit.) But the extensive damage has kept the place vacant ever since that day. Even in the months following the purchase of the site, when tensions rose over the ambitious plans of the developers to create a structure that might cast its shadow over the planned memorial where the World Trade Center had stood, few could be found to question the actual legal right of the property owners to do as they liked with the site. Nor were there any protests when modest Muslim prayer services began to be conducted there in late 2009.

But once the scale of the project became generally known, concern grew among the families of 9/11 victims and ordinary New Yorkers. Despite the mounting criticism of the scheme, approval was swiftly secured through the local community-planning board as well as the city's Landmarks Preservation Commission, which removed the final legal obstacle on August 3, 2010. Since the putative Islamic center was led by a figure well known in the world of interfaith dialogue, the rationale for the expeditious treatment of the proposal was seen as support for the idea put forward by Imam Abdul Rauf that the new building would be a symbol of tolerance.

But for whom was tolerance being sought? Though this avowal was cheered by liberal clergy of many faiths as well as some political figures, the signal being sent was that what was needed at or around Ground Zero was not so much remembrance of the attack on New York by Islamists *but a warning to Americans not to think ill of Muslims.*

It is this subtext of the plan for the center and mosque that has grated on the nerves of many Americans. They see the Ground Zero environs as a place whose only proper purpose ought to be one of national mourning—and a return to business activity that would stand as a defiant rejoinder to the destructive efforts of al-Qaeda. Moreover, the way in which the feelings of most of the families of 9/11 victims were discarded without much ado also fueled the fires of protest about the plan. It was on this point that the Anti-Defamation League [ADL], an organization as besotted with the concept of interfaith dialogue as any and whose largely liberal inclinations on domestic politics are well known, chose to speak out in favor of moving the center to a less contentious site. But rather than listen to the concerns of the ADL and the many other critics of the project, the backers of the project raised the ante, labeling the group and those who agreed with it as misguided bigots. It was at this point that Mayor Bloomberg issued his grandiose endorsement of the Islamic center, eschewing compromise as appeasement of prejudice.

It is true that in the heat of the debate, extreme views and statements that could well be interpreted as demeaning to all of Islam were soon expressed by a few of the protesters. But the test of goodwill applied here was soon revealed to be the same as the one CAIR seeks to enforce on other topics: any criticism of the mosque plan was quickly labeled as prejudice. When Rauf's previous statements rationalizing those who blamed American policy for 9/11 and a refusal to call Hamas a terrorist organization (always a pressure point for groups like CAIR because of its own history as a Hamas front) came to light, concerns that his moderation was more a matter of support for "progressive" politics than a genuine understanding of the threat from terrorism were similarly dismissed. Rather than engage with the other side, supporters of the project were unwilling to listen to or respect any opposing view.

Critics of the Islamic center were also accused of turning the topic into a political football, with Republicans Newt Gingrich and Sarah Palin widely slammed for rabble-rousing on the issue. But political gamesmanship on this topic was hardly limited to the right, as President Obama sought to establish himself as a defender of religious liberty by using the mosque—though the president backed away from his stand less than a day after delivering his own broadside at a White House Ramadan dinner. But no one in the anti-center camp disputed mosque construction anywhere but in the direct flight path of 9/11. And most mosque opponents were careful to point out that they did not deny the "right" of the site's owners to put up the mosque and center there, just the propriety of the move. If there was a political low point to the discussion, it was reached by House Speaker Nacy Pelosi, who threatened to investigate the funding of opponents of the center.

The Park51 Project Ignores the Victims of 9/11

By reframing the Ground Zero controversy as one in which the reasonable concerns of the vast majority of Americans were portrayed as bigoted, the organizers of the project and the Muslim organizations had scored a stunning victory. It may well be true that Abdul Rauf and his backers see the world very differently from al-Qaedas 9/11 murderers and do not intend their building to serve, as some critics fear, as a victory monument for Islam like the mosques built on the ruins of Judaisms Holy Temple in Jerusalem or' the minarets that adorn what was once St. Sophias Cathedral in Istanbul. But their mosque will be another kind of monument, one that serves to institutionalize a very different way of thinking about September 11.

Unlike planned memorials at Ground Zero that should serve to perpetuate the memory of the thousands of victims of 9/11 who perished at the hands of Islamist fanatics determined to pursue their war against the West, Park51's ultimate purpose will be to reinterpret that national tragedy in a way that will fundamentally distort that memory. The shift in the debate threatens to transmute 9/11 into a story of a strange one-off event that led to a mythical reign of domestic terror in which Muslims and their faith came under siege. It exempts every major branch of Islam from even the most remote connection to al-Qaeda and it casts the adherents of that faith as the ultimate sufferers of 9/11.

This account is an effort to redirect, redefine, and rewrite the unambiguous meaning of an unambiguous event. To achieve this aim, those who propound it are painting a vicious and libelous portrait of the United States and its citizens as hostile to and violent toward a minority population that was almost entirely left in peace and protected from any implication of involvement in the 9/11 crimes.

The conduct of the United States and its people toward Americans who profess Islam over the past nine years has been exemplary. The conduct of those who would build the mosque at Ground Zero, the Islamic organizations who have used the controversy to their advantage, and elitist opinion makers who have, in the course of this mess, suddenly discovered a passion for the free expression of religion and arrogantly set aside the sensibilities of those connected to the true victims of 9/11, has been the opposite of exemplary.

Being Opposed to the Islamic Cultural Center Is Not Being Islamophobic

Rich Noyes

Rich Noyes is research director at Media Reality Check.

By a wide margin—66 percent to 29 percent, according to the most recent [September 8, 2010] ABC News/ *Washington Post* poll—the public is opposed to building that proposed $100 million Islamic cultural center near the site of the destroyed World Trade Towers. This is not a lightly-held opinion: more than half (53%) told ABC news they are "strongly opposed" to building it near Ground Zero, vs. only 14 percent who report being "strongly" in favor.

The Public Is Opposed to the Islamic Cultural Center

So in the face of such obvious public sentiment, are the big broadcast networks reflecting such public sentiment in their coverage? Or are journalists implicitly repudiating their viewers by touting accusations that opposition to the mosque is motivated by America's supposed "Islamophobia"?

To find out, MRC [*Media Reality Check*] analysts reviewed all 52 stories about the Ground Zero mosque on the ABC, CBS and NBC evening newscasts from August 14 through September 13—the first month after President Obama propelled the issue into the headlines with his remarks at a White House dinner.

The results show that the networks have tilted in favor of mosque supporters and against public opinion, with more than half (55%) of all soundbites or reporter comments coming down on the pro-mosque side of the debate, vs. 45 percent for opponents.

Even those overall numbers fail to show how the debate has grown increasingly tilted over time. During the first week (August 14–20), the networks actually provided more visibility to mosque opponents—55 percent of soundbites, vs. 45 percent for mosque supporters. But in the following weeks (August 21 to September 13), the networks' coverage lurched in the other direction, with mosque supporters receiving a 63 percent to 37 percent advantage.

Our analysts tallied as "pro-mosque" all statements and soundbites that either: supported the idea of building the Islamic center on its currently proposed site; defended or praised the project's organizers (mainly the Imam Feisal Abdul Rauf); or criticized the other side as bigoted or "Islamophobic." Anti-mosque statements/soundbites presented the other side: criticized the plans to build the center and/or the project's organizers, or defended mosque opponents from charges of bigotry.

The Media Changed the Narrative to Bigotry

The shift in coverage occurred after mosque proponents began tarring their opponents as bigots. A pair of protests on Sunday, August 22—one in favor of the mosque, one against—drew coverage on all three network newscasts, and all three highlighted the accusation from pro-mosque demonstrators that a contrary stance was evidence of what *Time* magazine's cover story that week dubbed "Islamophobia."

What had been a relatively even-handed debate about balancing the sensitivities of 9/11 families with America's tradition of religious freedom morphed into a one-sided story about beleaguered Muslims facing hardship at the hands of bigoted Americans. On the August 23 *Nightly News*, for example, NBC's Ron Allen picked up how "many Muslim-Americans insist this debate is more evidence of religious intolerance."

On the August 25 *CBS Evening News*, fill-in anchor Jeff Glor linked the stabbing of a cab driver to the mosque debate: "That alleged hate crime took place in the shadow of a heated and divisive debate over whether a mosque should be built near Ground Zero. . . . Other controversies over new mosques in Wisconsin and Kentucky have led some to question: Is America becoming Islamophobic, a prejudice against Muslims?"

Four days later, on ABC's *World News*, correspondent Steve Osunsami cited "a string of recent incidents suggesting that many Americans don't care for Muslims—the back and forth over the Islamic center near Ground Zero, the cab driver who was stabbed simply for being Muslim."

"Critics say all the rhetoric is fueling anti-Muslim violence," ABC's Dan Harris chimed in on the September 5 *World News*.

ABC and CBS both touted exclusive interviews with organizers of the Ground Zero mosque project, but never gave the same privilege to mosque opponents. These interviews were hardly probing. CBS's Scott Pelley interviewed Sharif el-Gamal, the real estate developer who bought the property two blocks from Ground Zero, excerpts of which were shown on the August 27 and August 30 *Evening News*.

"This facility that is being debated all around the world is universally known as the Ground Zero mosque," Pelley told el-Gamal. "What do you call it?"

"It should be universally known as a hub of culture, a hub of co-existence, a hub of bringing people together," el-Gamal enthused.

ABC's Christiane Amanpour interviewed Abdul Rauf for the September 12 *This Week*, with excerpts shown on the September 9 *World News*. She quoted Abdul Rauf as arguing that failing to proceed with his mosque concept would "strengthen the radicals in the Muslim world, help their recruitment. This will put our people, our soldiers, our troops, our embassies, our citizens, under attack in the Muslim world. And we have expanded and given and fueled terrorism."

CAIR is currently listed by federal prosecutors as an unindicted co-conspirator in their investigation of funding for Middle Eastern terrorist groups such as Hamas.

Seemingly deaf to what she just heard, Amanpour characterized Abdul Rauf's statement this way: "So, he said he wasn't making any threats or predicting any terrible worst case scenario."

Alone among the three evening newscasts, ABC's *World News* also offered soundbites to Ibrahim Hooper, a spokesman for the Council on American Islamic Relations (CAIR) to propose that Americans were prejudiced against Muslims. (NBC's *Today* on September 9 also featured a CAIR representative to speak out against Americans as bigoted.) CAIR is currently listed by federal prosecutors as an unindicted co-conspirator in their investigation of funding for Middle Eastern terrorist groups such as Hamas.

Newscasters Exaggerated the Level of Islamophobia

"I've really never seen the level of Islamophobia that we're experiencing today," Hooper blasted on the August 16 *World News*, a soundbite that was repeated on the August 29 broadcast. A week later, on the September 5 *World News*, Hooper was back to condemn the "hysterical atmosphere we're in right now."

Parsing the numbers a different way provides some insight into how the networks seem to conceptualize the issue of balance: Debate about the Islamic center itself and/or its organizers was almost perfectly balanced (57 soundbites arguing against the project, vs. 54 soundbites in favor, or a 51–49% split). But the "debate" about whether opposition reflected Islamophobia was almost perfectly one-sided: 27 soundbites (93%) leveling that accusation, with just two soundbites (7%) offering a defense.

In other words, the networks permitted a balanced debate about a proposed real estate project, but allowed mosque supporters to attack the majority of Americans as "haters" and "bigots" without adequate debate.

That's yet another sign that the liberal, elite media are hopelessly out of touch with the public they ostensibly serve.

False Charges of Islamophobia Are Being Used by Radical Groups to Advance Their Cause

Robert Spencer

Robert Spencer, an American author and blogger, is the director of Jihad Watch and is best known for critiques of Islam.

"The Muslim world is going through an unprecedented difficult and trying time," said the Secretary General of the 56-state Organization of the Islamic Conference [OIC], Ekmeleddin Ihsanoglu, on Friday [September 24, 2010].

One might reasonably have thought that he was referring to the recent increase in violent jihad [holy war] incidents in the West, perpetrated by Muslims who explained and justified their actions by reference to Islamic texts and teachings. But no, Ihsanoglu was exercised about "Islamophobia," the invented term Islamic supremacists use to try to stifle realistic analysis of the global jihad in all its manifestations.

The Real Issue Is Islamic Violence, Not Free Speech

"We are facing daunting challenges and severe hardships," Ihsanoglu complained. "Islam and Muslims are under serious attack, and Islamophobia is growing and becoming more rampant and dangerous by the day."

It is not at all established that "Islamophobia" really is growing. In fact, the FBI [Federal Bureau of Investigation] has recently released data establishing that hate crimes against Muslims are comparatively rare. But if there is any actual suspicion of or negative feelings toward Muslims in the United States, it is solely and wholly the responsibility of Nidal Hasan, the Fort Hood [Texas] jihadist; Umar Farouk Abdulmutallab, the Christmas underwear jihadist; Abdulhakim Mujahid Muhammad, who killed one soldier and murdered another in a jihad shooting outside a military recruiting station in Little Rock, Ark.; Faisal Shahzad, the Times Square jihadist; Khaled Sheikh Mohammed and Osama bin Laden on 9/11; the London jihad bombers of July 7, 2005; and so many others.

What Ihsanoglu and the OIC want Western states to do is limit the freedom of speech regarding Islam and jihad.

Yet Ihsanoglu, with an evasion of responsibility that is characteristic of Islamic supremacists, pretends that non-Muslims are growing more suspicious of Muslims and Islam not because of this, but because of some gratuitous bigotry. This is a tried and tested tactic, designed precisely to divert attention from Islamic jihad attacks and to shame and discredit those who would dare stand up to jihad (both violent and stealth) and Islamic supremacism in the West.

Without any reference to the pandemic of jihad violence either in the U.S. or worldwide, Ihsanoglu referred instead to a "pandemic of Islam vilification" in the U.S. and Europe, and declared: "We need an all inclusive effort of OIC member states to stem this menace. That is why I firmly believe that this question of Islamophobia should figure prominently on the agenda of all OIC member states whenever they deal with their Western counterparts."

What Ihsanoglu and the OIC want Western states to do is limit the freedom of speech regarding Islam and jihad. In 2008 he issued a dictatorial warning: "We sent a clear message to the West regarding the red lines that should not be crossed" regarding free speech about Islam and terrorism. And he reported success: "The official West and its public opinion are all now well-aware of the sensitivities of these issues. They have also started to look seriously into the question of freedom of expression from the perspective of its inherent responsibility, which should not be overlooked."

Since then he has encountered success beyond his wildest dreams, for the [Barack] Obama Administration has extended and broadened the [George W.] Bush policy of refraining from speaking about Islam and jihad in connection with acts of Islamic jihad terrorism. The absurdity of this policy reached its apex with the official report on the Fort Hood massacre, which blithely ignored Nidal Hasan's clear, public, and repeated adherence to Islamic jihad doctrine, his cries of "Allahu akbar" as he committed his murders, and his passing out of Korans on the morning of his massacre.

Ihsanoglu is coming to Chicago for a conference with leaders of [terrorist organization] Hamas-linked groups such as the Council on American-Islamic Relations (CAIR) and the Islamic Society of North America (ISNA). The mainstream media will almost certainly overlook the principal importance of the conference, and its anti-free speech agenda, and will report uncritically about the rise in "Islamophobia" and the fears among Muslims of a "backlash." There will be no discussion at this conference of how to prevent or even limit the spread of the jihad ideology among Muslims—in other words, there will be no attempt to attack the actual causes of "Islamophobia."

In less Orwellian [referring to George Orwell's novel *Nineteen Eighty-Four*] times, that would be revealing enough for anyone to see how the Organization of the Islamic Conference and its allies are using charges of "Islamophobia" as a weapon to advance the jihad no less unmistakably than Osama bin Laden did on September 11, 2001.

Current
CONTROVERSIES

CHAPTER 3

Is Suspicion of Islam Rational?

Overview: Both Conservatives and Liberals Have Valid Arguments About Islam

Cathy Young

Cathy Young is a contributing editor at Reason *magazine and columnist at RealClearPolitics.*

In March [2011], almost 10 years after the attacks of September 11, 2001, America's uneasy, contradictory relationship with Islam was on full display at two congressional hearings. The first, a House Committee on Homeland Security meeting chaired by Rep. Peter King (R-N.Y.), tackled "radicalization" among American Muslims. Three weeks later, Senate Majority Whip Dick Durbin (D-Ill.) presided over a Senate Judiciary Committee panel that heard testimony about anti-Muslim prejudice. Conservatives trumpet the Muslim peril, while liberals warn of Islamophobia.

Islamic extremism is indeed a serious global problem today, to a degree unmatched by the radical fringes of other major religions. While violent fundamentalism is far less of a problem in the United States than in many other parts of the world, radicalism within the American Muslim community is not entirely an invention of the Islamophobic right. The 2009 Fort Hood [Texas] shooting by U.S. Army Major Nidal Malik Hasan is an extreme but real example of what some Americans are willing to do. And a 2007 Pew poll found that 27 percent of American Muslim men under 30 believe suicide terrorism in defense of Islam is at least sometimes justified.

Cathy Young, "Fear of a Muslim America: In the Fight Against Radical Islam, Conservatives Are Trying to Limit the Property and Speech Rights of Peaceful American Muslims," *Reason*, Vol. 43, No. 4, August-September 2011, p. 20. Copyright © 2010 by Reason. All rights reserved. Reproduced by permission.

But bias against American Muslims isn't a P.C. [politically correct] myth. Once confined mainly to a few rightwing blogs, anti-Islamic bigotry has become a visible presence in Republican politics and the respectable conservative media. All around the country, right-of-center activists and politicians are trying to use government force to limit the property rights of Muslims and repel the alleged menace of Shariah [Islamic] law. Islamophobia has crossed the line from fringe rhetorical hysteria to active discrimination against U.S. citizens of the Islamic faith. . . .

Culture Clash

There are real cultural conflicts involving the practice of Islamic beliefs in the United States. At the extreme, these tensions can escalate into severe and even deadly violence toward women who transgress traditional norms of behavior. Far more commonly, disputes have arisen over such minor yet momentarily divisive issues as cab drivers turning down passengers who are carrying alcoholic beverages or accompanied by service dogs. (In many such cases, the "Muslim" position is a fringe one within Islam. While Muslims are forbidden to drink alcohol and strongly discouraged from keeping dogs as house pets, most Islamic authorities agree there is no prohibition on transporting either.)

So far the official responses to these disputes show no signs of a rush to either appeasement or persecution. In Minneapolis-St. Paul, the only metropolitan area where taxi drivers' denial of service to liquor-carrying passengers at the airport is a significant issue, the city responded with stiff penalties—a 30-day license suspension on the first offense, a two-year revocation on the second—for refusing a passenger for "unwarranted reasons."

In other instances, furor over Islamization has been set off by trivial and harmless measures that infringe on no one's rights, such as the installation on a few college campuses of foot baths for Muslim students to use for ritual ablutions. Such provisions are no different in principle from accommodations that benefit other religious groups, such as kosher menus in student dining halls. . . .

Nor is there anything new about conflicts and controversies over religion and state. In upstate New York in the 1980s, parents in an Orthodox Jewish enclave sued the public school board because of their objections to female drivers on school buses carrying boys; when the suit was rejected, they created their own school district, which was green-lit by the state legislature but later blocked by the U.S. Supreme Court as overly religious in nature. In some religious communities that expect all interpersonal disputes to be handled by spiritual elders—Jehovah's Witnesses, ultraOrthodox Jews, the Amish—there have been serious concerns about cover-ups of criminal acts such as child sexual abuse, because of traditional pressure to not report such crimes to the secular authorities.

The hard-to-swallow truth is that anti-Islam polemicists have a point: Islam is not quite the same as any other major religion.

How do critics of "Islamization" deal with these parallels? Last December, a Jewish reader on the website of Middle East Forum Director Daniel Pipes pointed out that much-reviled proposals to allow Muslims to voluntarily settle domestic relations cases and financial disputes in Shariah courts are analogous to existing Jewish religious courts or within-community conflict resolutions among Mormons or the Amish. Pipes responded: "Jews and Amish do not try to take over the United States; Islamists do." Thus, all Muslims who ask for modest and standard accommodations for their religious values are equated with "Islamists" who seek to take over America, and any concessions to such requests are seen as "the camel's nose under the tent"—the first step to public floggings, stonings, and beheadings.

Any accommodation of faith-based beliefs that violates fundamental liberties and individual rights should be firmly rejected, whether it's the acceptance of religiously sanctioned wife beating or the recent suggestion by Washburn University law professor Liaquat Ali Khan that "desecrations of the Qur'an" should be outlawed because "given the presence of a growing population of American Muslims, Qur'an burning threatens domestic peace." But the anti-Islamic backlash threatens essential rights too. Efforts to block the construction of mosques using government muscle are the most obvious example. The recent Shariah bans could prevent American courts from honoring and enforcing private contracts and agreements based on Islamic religious law, and perhaps even from recognizing the validity of marriages performed by Islamic courts abroad.

The Myth of the Muslim Monolith

The hard-to-swallow truth is that anti-Islam polemicists have a point: Islam is not quite the same as any other major religion. There is no country in the world right now where a Christian or Jewish government executes people for blasphemy, apostasy, or illicit sex; several major Muslim states do. Earlier this year in Pakistan, after Punjab Gov. Salman Taseer spoke out in defense of a Christian woman sentenced to death for allegedly insulting Muhammad, Taseer himself was murdered. Large segments of the Pakistani public, including politicians and clerics, hailed his assassin as a hero. Even in modernized Malaysia and Indonesia, which have legal guarantees for religious minorities and are often cited as models of tolerance among majority-Muslim states, Shariah courts have the de facto power to bar any Muslim from converting to another faith or (for women) marrying a non-Muslim.

But many self-styled anti-jihadists [people opposed to combatants in a holy war]—[Pamela] Geller, her guru and comrade-in-arms Robert Spencer, Michelle Malkin, and quite a few others—go further, claiming that fanaticism, intolerance, and violence are at the core of Islam and that the religion is impervious to reform. Spencer, who blogs at Jihad Watch.org, adamantly asserts that terrorism is the real face of Islam and that so-called moderate Muslims are either liars or dupes who don't understand the true nature of their faith. As evidence, he and others quote inflammatory verses from the Koran that prescribe the conquest and slaughter of unbelievers and enjoin the faithful against befriending Christians and Jews.

Yet the Bible has more than a few alarmingly violent and intolerant passages, and even the relatively pacific New Testament contains an exhortation from St. Paul to avoid friendships with non-Christians. Such verses have not prevented most Christians from coming to terms with modernity and liberal democracy. Much more of Islam is stuck in a premodern, authoritarian frame of mind. When a figure like Sheik Yusuf al-Qaradawi—the Qatar-based cleric who advocates capital punishment for apostates and homosexuals and the "light beating" of unruly wives—can be an esteemed religious scholar and a reputed "moderate" it says a great deal about the current state of the religion.

But there are many Muslims who have condemned and stood up against terrorism, including those who recently volunteered to serve as human shields for Christian churches in Egypt after church bombings by Islamist fanatics. There are Muslim scholars who are advocating a revision of Islamic orthodoxy on issues ranging from women's rights to blasphemy and apostasy, and who are challenging the age-old clerical doctrine that the Koran's earlier, more peaceful and tolerant verses are nullified by the later, more militant ones. In 2004, over 2,500 Muslim academics from 23 countries signed a petition condemning "theologians of terror" (al-Qaradawi among them) who use Islamic scriptures as justification for political violence. It remains to be seen whether such voices will prevail in the Arab Spring sweeping the Middle East.

Islamist radicalism is pervasive enough to pose thorny problems for the West. Even in the United States, where the Muslim community is far more integrated into the mainstream culture than in Europe, some mosques have been used for terrorist recruitment and some supposedly moderate Muslim groups have provided a platform to those who advocate violence. . . .

With Muslims accounting for nearly a quarter of the world's population, the modernization of Islam is one of the 21st century's most urgent priorities. But the obstacles to reform come not only from militant Islamism but from Islamophobia as well. The Islamophobes, after all, repeat everything the Islamists tell Muslims: that the West is implacably hostile to them and their faith, that the most extreme and violent form of Islam is also its truest form, and that a liberalized Islam is impossible. American Muslims, and America, deserve better.

Fundamentalist Muslims Are Violent and Pose a Real Threat

Andrew C. McCarthy

Andrew C. McCarthy is a senior fellow at the National Review Institute and the author of several books, including The Grand Jihad: How Islam and the Left Sabotage America.

"From a purely academic point of view, this translation is superior to anything produced by orientalists in the way of translations of major Islamic works." Taha Jabir al-Alwani was writing about *Reliance of the Traveller*, the English version of *Umdat al-Salik*, the classic manual of sharia ("Islamic Sacred Law," as the cover of *Reliance* puts it). Alwani is no lightweight in these matters. His specialty is *fiqh*—Islamic jurisprudence. In fact, he has been a member of the Islamic Fiqh Academy in Saudi Arabia and is renowned among orientalist scholars in the West as president of the Fiqh Council of North America.

Concern About the Actions of Islamists Is Rational

More significant, he was writing in his capacity as president of the International Institute of Islamic Thought (IIIT). Head-quartered in Virginia, IIIT is an Islamist think tank created by the Muslim Brotherhood in the early 1980s.

I was reminded of Dr. Alwani when reading the latest hit job against my friends David Horowitz and Robert Spencer, authored by the Center for American Progress [CAP]. Directed by [Bill] Clinton White House chief of staff John Podesta, CAP is a lushly financed leftist think tank that profoundly influences the [Barack] Obama administration—indeed, Podesta oversaw the Obama transition after the 2008 election. CAP's sugar daddy, George Soros, has made a cottage industry out of whitewashing Islamist ideology. This enterprise has lately produced a lengthy ad hominem rant called "Fear, Inc.: The Roots of the Islamophobia Network in America."

Islamophobia is a neologism coined by the Muslim Brotherhood, which is as practiced at the art of deception as any organization on Earth. It should come as no surprise, then, that Islamophobia is a smear, intended to discredit a phenomenon that, in truth, is neither a phobia—i.e., an irrational fear—nor concerned about Islam in general. The phenomenon, instead, is a quite rational disquiet about *Islamists*—fundamentalist Muslims, some of whom are violent jihadists and some stealth jihadists. They seek incrementally to implant sharia [Islamic law] principles in the West.

Islamist organizations abound in the United States. Like IIIT, many of them are affiliated with the Brotherhood and collaborate regularly with leftist organizations such as CAP. Reciprocally, CAP, like many in the Obama administration, advocates the Brotherhood's acceptance as a legitimate political party.

The Islamist groups purport to speak for the broader American Muslim community, but this is about as true as the claim that Occupy Wall Street speaks for 99 percent of Americans. Nevertheless, Islamist groups punch way above their weight, because they are lavishly financed, and they get red-carpet treatment from government officials—a bad habit the Obama administration has exacerbated but certainly did not originate.

Islamists Seek to Destroy Western Civilization

As I outlined in *The Grand Jihad: How Islam and the Left Sabotage America*, the Muslim Brotherhood is engaged in a "civilizational jihad" against America, Europe, and Israel. There is no need to take my word for it: Islamists are quite blunt about this fact when they speak among themselves. The title of my book, in fact, is drawn from the words of an internal Brotherhood communiqué seized by the FBI [Federal Bureau of Investigation], a memo in which the Brothers describe their work in America as a "grand jihad" aimed at "eliminating and destroying the Western civilization from within and 'sabotaging' its miserable house by their hands and the hands of the believers so that it is eliminated and God's religion is made victorious over all other religions."

It is no secret that the Brothers intend, as their leading jurisprudent, Sheikh Yusuf Qaradawi, puts it, to "conquer America" and "conquer Europe." Moreover, they believe this can be done mostly without violence, through a sedulous campaign of voluntary apartheid (integrating with but not assimilating into the West) and the infiltration of sharia principles into our law and our institutions. One need only open one's eyes to see that Islamists are acting on these intentions, and one need only glance at Europe to know that their strategy can work.

There is nothing phobic about being concerned over this. And although Islamist ideology is undeniably a mainstream interpretation of Islam in many Islamic countries, that is not the case in the United States—or, for that matter, in Indonesia, the largest Muslim country in the world by population. Contrary to the Brotherhood smear that the Left blithely retails, justifiable anxiety over the Brotherhood's designs is not a generalized fear of Muslims.

Naturally, this does not stop the CAP report from liberally applying the "Islamophobe" smear to Horowitz, Spencer, and other conservative commentators. I'm also mentioned in the report, something I learned about only a couple of days ago, when the castigation of Horowitz and Spencer was brought to my attention. Ordinarily, I'd sit through an Obama speech on

Solyndra's solar-bright future before I'd waste my time reading a Soros-funded report about a Soros hobby-horse. But David and Robert did read it, and responded forcefully. That prompted a reply from CAP's Matthew Duss, a co-author of the "Fear, Inc." report.

Duss's screed is the CAP report in small compass: long on character assassination, short on substance, disingenuous in relating its targets' position on Islam (as opposed to Islamist ideology), and woefully incomplete on Islamic scripture. That's to be expected, and I'm sure it will be a big hit at the many confabs where Islamists and leftists gather. More offensive is CAP's plea that *National Review* [NR] go lefty and turn Horowitz and Spencer into non-persons. CAP is basically the Obama administration's brain—where could NR and the Right possibly get more well-meaning advice about who should have credibility in our movement?

Our government could not have thwarted terrorist attacks without the assistance of patriotic Muslims.

As precedent, Duss purports to rely on Bill Buckley's famed ejection of the Birchers. The comparison is noxious, but typical. It was only a few years ago that a CAP offshoot ("Campus Progress") absurdly slandered Horowitz as a racist because he, like the vast majority of Americans, was opposed to the notion that Americans who had nothing to do with slavery should pay slavery reparations to people who were never slaves, 137 years after the abolition of slavery. (CAP might have considered stepping up to the plate for those still living in slavery in Saudi Arabia and Sudan, Islamic countries where the Koran's express approval of slavery enables the institution to endure.)

Horowitz, of course, is a former radical leftist who became a conservative of singular eloquence. With his intimate knowledge of how the progressive project works, David is his era's most consequential detractor of the Left, which has only slightly less contempt for its apostates than does Islam (on which more momentarily). Spencer, the longtime director of the invaluable Jihad Watch, is a scholar of sharia who works tirelessly to expose the global Islamist threat and to track the sundry collaborations of Islamists and leftists. To equate their carefully documented, amply supported critiques of Islamism to Robert Welch's lunatic claim that Dwight Eisenhower was a closet Communist is contemptible.

Islamists Promote Fundamentalist Sharia Law

It is not my burden to refute what Duss has said about Horowitz and Spencer. As one would expect, they have done that ably. . . . Nor is there benefit in spending much time on what Duss claims is "the actual argument made in 'Fear, Inc.,' which is that they, along with a small cadre of self-appointed experts and activists, promote the idea that religiously inspired terrorism represents true Islam." I have said any number of times that I do not presume to say what "true Islam" is, or even if there is a single true Islam. What the true Islam may be is irrelevant to U.S. national security; what matters is that Islamist ideology—which fuels both the terrorist threat and the Muslim Brotherhood's multi-faceted civilizational jihad—is a mainstream construction of Islam to which many millions of Muslims adhere. If they believe it and act on it, it is a threat regardless of whether it is an authentic expression of "true Islam."

I've pointedly and repeatedly observed that our government could not have thwarted terrorist attacks without the assistance of patriotic Muslims who've worked against the violent jihadists. And, like Horowitz and Spencer, I regularly use the term "Islamist" rather than "Islam" to draw a distinction between the ideology of the enemy and Islam as it is practiced by most American Muslims, and by millions of Muslims throughout the world. We can make a sober concession that Islamist ideology draws on Islamic scripture without leaping to the conclusion that it is the only legitimate interpretation of Islamic scripture.

The most risible aspect of CAP's Islamophobia smear is that it cavalierly sells out the Muslims it pretends to defend. As the commentators CAP vilifies are wont to point out, among the most persecuted victims of Islamist ideology are Muslim women, Muslim homosexuals, and patriotic American Muslims who, in the tradition of *E Pluribus Unum* [out of many, one], want to empower their fellow Muslims to assimilate and enjoy Western civil-rights norms—in sharp contrast to Islamists, who regard encouraging Muslims to assimilate in the West as a "crime against humanity." Duss, however, tells us not to worry about sharia's compatibility with "a modern society," because its more unsavory features are not reflected in the practice of Islam by most American Muslims, whom Duss describes as "Sharia-adherent."

"Jihad means to war against non-Muslims"

Of course, the problem is that American Muslims are being encouraged (and in some cases, coerced) into fundamentalist sharia—to which most of them are certainly not adherent—by Muslim Brotherhood organizations such as IIIT, which CAP is abetting, whether knowingly or not. . . . That brings us back to Dr. Alwani and the English translation of *Reliance of the Traveller*.

The IIIT president's lavish praise for the translation, which he called an "eminent work of Islamic jurisprudence," was not idle. It was written in an IIIT report that is included in the preface of *Reliance* as an endorsement of the manual's rendering of sharia. The purpose of the translation, Alwani explained, is to make this faithful interpretation of sharia "accessible" to English speakers who are not fluent in the original Arabic. "The book will be of great use," he elaborated, "in America,

Britain, and Canada," among other countries. Echoing IIIT's commendation is the certification that immediately follows from the Islamic Research Academy at al-Azhar University in Cairo, the ancient and profoundly influential seat of Sunni learning.

The Precepts of Sharia Law Are Frightening

The manual is startling. To take just a few of its innumerable bracing instructions, it pronounces that:

- Apostasy from Islam is "the ugliest form of unbelief" for which the penalty is death ("When a person who has reached puberty and is sane voluntarily apostatizes from Islam, he deserves to be killed")

- Apostasy occurs not only when a Muslim renounces Islam but also, among other things, when a Muslim appears to worship an idol, when he is heard "to speak words that imply unbelief," when he makes statements that appear to deny or revile Allah or the prophet Mohammed, when he is heard "to deny the obligatory character of something which by consensus of Muslims is part of Islam," and when he is heard "to be sarcastic about any ruling of the Sacred Law"

- "Jihad means to war against non-Muslims"

- Non-Muslims are permitted to live in an Islamic state only if they follow the rules of Islam, pay the non-Muslim poll tax, and comply with various adhesive conditions designed to remind them that they have been subdued (such as wearing distinctive clothing, keeping to one side of the street, not being greeted with "Peace be with you" ("*as-Salamu alaykum*"), not being permitted to build as high as or higher than Muslims, and being forbidden to build new churches, recite prayers aloud, "or make public displays of their funerals or feast days"

- Offenses committed against Muslims (including murder) are more serious than offenses committed against non-Muslims

- The penalty for spying against Muslims is death

- The penalty for fornication is to be stoned to death, unless one is without the "capacity to remain chaste," in which case the penalty is "being scourged one hundred stripes and banished to a distance of at least 81 km./ 50mi. for one year"

- The penalty for homosexual activity ("sodomy and lesbianism") is death

- A Muslim woman may only marry a Muslim man; a Muslim man may marry up to four women, who may be Muslim, Christian, or Jewish (but no apostates from Islam)

- A woman is required to be obedient to her husband and is prohibited from leaving the marital home without permission; if permitted to go out, she must conceal her figure or alter it "to a form unlikely to draw looks from men or attract them"

- A non-Muslim may not be awarded custody of a Muslim child

- The penalty for theft is amputation of the right hand

- The penalty for drinking alcohol is "to be scourged forty stripes"

- The penalty for accepting interest ("usurious gain") is death (i.e., to be considered in a state of war against Allah)

- The testimony of a woman is worth half that of a man

- If a case involves an allegation of fornication (including rape), "then it requires four male witnesses"

- The establishment of a caliphate is obligatory, and the caliph must be Muslim and male

Most American Muslims Reject Sharia Law

The IIIT was established by Muslim Brotherhood figures in 1980. Its mission is the Islamization of knowledge—"a new synthesis of all knowledge in an Islamic epistemological framework," as recounted in an important study, "The Muslim Brotherhood in the United States," authored by the Hudson Institute's Center on Islam, Democracy, and the Future of the Muslim World. As I've previously explained, the Brotherhood expressly identified the IIIT as being among "our organizations and the organizations of our friends" in internal memoranda seized by the FBI and admitted in evidence at the [terrorist organization] Hamas-financing trial. It shares common leaders with the Islamic Society of North America, another Brotherhood affiliate that was shown to be complicit in the Hamas-financing conspiracy. And Dr. Alwani himself was cited as an unindicted coconspirator in the Justice Department's prosecution against Palestinian Islamic Jihad leader Sami al-Arian, who ultimately pleaded guilty to a terrorism charge.

The IIIT's sharia—the one it labors to make more "accessible"—is not the form of Islam that American Muslims appear to desire. In fact, its gradual adoption, which the publication of *Reliance* was designed to facilitate, would make life incalculably worse for American Muslims. That is a fact of the sort that, for years, David Horowitz and Robert Spencer have taken many a sling and arrow to expose. It is a fact the Center for American Progress prefers to obscure. I doubt that factophobia will prove a winning strategy, either for American Muslims or for American national security.

Islamic Supremacists Pose a Clear and Present Danger

Mark Tapson

Mark Tapson is a screenwriter and commentator on politics and popular culture for FrontPage, Big Hollywood, Pajamas Media, Townhall, Big Peace, *and elsewhere. He is a Shillman Journalism fellow at the David Horowitz Freedom Center.*

The recently released report "Fear, Inc.: The Roots of the Islamophobia Network in America," from the George Soros-funded Center for American Progress (CAP), purports to expose a sinister network of American "Islamophobes" funded by a "flood of cash" who manufacture conspiracy theories about Islam, spread hate and bigotry against all Muslim-Americans, and inspire violence toward them, all for financial and political gain. But in fact, the very concept of Islamophobia is manufactured propaganda used by the subversive Muslim Brotherhood and their leftist support network to demonize and silence critics of Islamic fundamentalism. . . .

Although there are dozens and dozens of serious, qualified critics of Muslim fundamentalism, the report hones in on five figures it deems to be the central nervous system of this "Islamophobic" network:

- Frank Gaffney at the Center for Security Policy.

- David Yerushalmi at the Society of Americans for National Existence.

- Daniel Pipes at the Middle East Forum.

- Robert Spencer of Jihad Watch and Stop Islamization of America.

- Steven Emerson of the Investigative Project on Terrorism.

The report's methodology consists almost entirely of its authors painting their targets as sinister, conspiratorial bigots.

The report also targets other perpetrators whom they label "the validators" and "the activists," as well as miscellaneous "misinformation experts," "political players," "right-wing media," and "grassroots organizations and the religious right."...

The authors of the report claim that "due in part to the relentless efforts of this small group of individuals and organizations, Islam is now the most negatively viewed religion in America." Some of that negativity may indeed stem from these individuals and organizations educating people about unsettling aspects of Islam that they were unaware of before, aspects that contradict the Left's (and many on the Right's) mantra that Islam is a Religion of Peace.

Manufacturing "Islamophobia"

Far from being unbiased or even seriously investigative, the report's methodology consists almost entirely of its authors painting their targets as sinister, conspiratorial bigots rather than addressing the substance of their arguments. Contrary to the authors' own claim that they reject "shrill, fear-based attacks" and desire a "fact-based civil discourse," the report is packed with ugly terminology designed 1) to demonize these falsely labeled "Islamophobes" as a "small band of radical ideologues" and "misinformation experts" who are intentionally "mischaracterizing Islam," "peddling hate and fear of Muslims," and "raving" of the "overhyped dangers" of Sharia [Islamic law], and 2) to dismiss their work, which is described repeatedly as "sinister," "hateful," "purposively deceptive," "bigoted," "racist," and the like.

Note, for example, the report's insistent use of the label "anti-Muslim," a slur which automatically designates anyone trying to educate others about the very real threat of global jihad [holy war] as a mere bigot. . . .

In addition to "anti-Muslim," the report makes many dozens of references to Islamophobia, which it defines as "an exaggerated fear, hatred, and hostility toward Islam and Muslims that is perpetuated by negative stereotypes resulting in bias, discrimination, and the marginalization and exclusion of Muslims from America's social, political, and civic life." (The authors don't address the possibility that much of what they consider Islamophobia might simply be a perfectly rational, legitimate concern about the clear and present danger of Islamic supremacism.). . .

Breivik bombed a government building in Oslo and proceeded to murder many dozens of teens at a nearby youth camp.

Predictably, the specter of McCarthyism [Senator Joseph McCarthy conducted anti-communist hearings in the 1950s] is raised in the report as well, in a specious attempt to link the abovementioned anti-jihadists to "some of the darkest episodes in American history, in which religious, ethnic, and racial minorities were discriminated against and persecuted." Addressing the threat of Islamic fundamentalism is not the same as persecuting all Muslims; indeed, "Fear, Inc." notes that the majority of victims of Islamic extremists have been Muslims themselves. Therefore, by being at the forefront of the effort to identify and confront the militants, the report's five "Islamophobes" and others in their "network" are actually *de-*

fending non-militant Muslims—unlike the authors of the report, who are enabling the fundamentalists.

In addition to the false charge of McCarthyism, Ed Lasky at *American Thinker* and Daniel Greenfield in his own article point out that the report is buoyed by an undercurrent of anti-Semitism, stoking "the view that rich Jews operate behind the scenes and use their wealth to control the media and government policy."

Another demonizing tactic recurring throughout the report is the slanderous connection the authors attempt to draw between their targets and Norwegian terrorist Anders Breivik. In July, Breivik bombed a government building in Oslo [Norway] and proceeded to murder many dozens of teens at a nearby youth camp, which was attended by the children of leftwing politicians whom he blamed for facilitating the Islamization of the West. The authors of the report waste no time trying to link him repeatedly to their targets; in fact, the report *begins* with a description of Breivik's assault.

Breivik left behind a 1500-page manifesto which, as the authors of the report point out *ad infinitum* [to infinity], cites the names and work of some of the "Islamophobes" they seek to smear:

> Based on Breivik's sheer number of citations and references to the writings of these individuals, it is clear that he read and relied on the hateful, anti-Muslim ideology of a number of men and women detailed in this report . . .

> While these bloggers and pundits were not responsible for Breivik's deadly attacks, their writings on Islam and multiculturalism appear to have helped create a world view, held by this lone Norwegian gunman, that sees Islam as at war with the West and the West needing to be defended.

The authors of the report know that they can't blame the "Islamophobes" directly for the attacks, so they attempt to pin the murders on them in some vague way for having created "a negative world view" of Islam. This conveniently overlooks the glaringly obvious fact that *it is the Islamic supremacists themselves, not their critics, who have created this world view*. But it suits the authors' agenda to ignore the Islamists' many pronouncements that they *are* at war with the West, and to shoot the messengers instead.

The report begins with the intentionally misleading claim that Breivik cited scholar of Islam and Director of Jihad Watch Robert Spencer 162 times in his ramblings. In fact, as Daniel Greenfield notes, "Breivik's 1,500-page manifesto had pasted in hundreds of documents, one of which was an independently assembled collection of quotes from Spencer, Tony Blair and others on Islam." In other words, most of those 162 "citations" came from a document Breivik didn't even write, inserted into his own. . . .

The report also rarely addresses the legitimate concerns raised by the anti-jihadists. The authors merely characterize the anti-jihadists' assertions as "misleading," "inaccurate," and "perverse" "fear-mongering"—without detailing *how* the supposed "Islamophobes" are wrong.

For example, the report states that its five principals are guilty of promoting "the deeply mistaken portrayal of Islam—a religion of nearly 1.6 billion people worldwide, including 2.6 million Americans—as an inherently violent ideology that seeks domination over the United States and all non-Muslims":

> Spencer neatly sums up their inaccurate and perverse view of Islam as "the only religion in the world that has a developed doctrine, theology and legal system that mandates violence against unbelievers and mandates that Muslims must wage war in order to establish the hegemony of the Islamic social order all over the world."

How is this view inaccurate and perverse? The report's authors do not explain; much less do they refute Spencer's "deeply mistaken portrayal" with sourced arguments to the contrary. Spencer's portrayal of Islam, on the other hand, derives from the Quran, the hadith, and the principal schools of Islamic jurisprudence in authority today. He replies:

> [I]t is a matter of objective verification that all the mainstream Islamic sects and schools of Islamic jurisprudence do indeed teach that the Islamic *umma* [community of nations] must wage war against unbelievers and subjugate them under the rule of Islamic law. The report does not and cannot produce any evidence that Islam does not contain sects and schools that teach this.

Activist groups . . . [seek] to advance progressive agendas, elect progressive candidates, and steer the Democratic Party ever-further towards the Left.

Rather than provide that evidence, which would publicly and definitively discredit the "Islamophobes" and correct their supposed misportrayal of Islam, the report's authors simply smear Spencer and the others as bigoted. They fall back on this tactic time and again throughout the report. So much for "fact-based civil discourse."

Funding

First comes a chapter on funding, designed to leave readers shocked, *shocked*, that non-profit organizations receive funds from donors and that people there get paid for their work. Or as Daniel Greenfield puts it: "In a staggering expose, the Center for American Progress has released a 130-page report revealing that organizations which investigate Islamic radicalism are funded by money, not sunshine." He notes that "the Center for American Progress' campaign for donor transparency, however, stops at its own doors. While its own budget is many times that of the organizations that its report targets—the CAP's policy is to keep the identities of its own donors secret."

"Fear, Inc." closes by acknowledging that it "was supported in part by a grant from the Open Society Foundations," the most prominent of the numerous foundations belonging to the international billionaire financier George Soros. Although the Center for American Progress describes itself as "a non-partisan research and educational institute," it is part of the administrative core of Soros's "Shadow Party," the network of non-profit activist groups organized by Soros and others to mobilize resources to advance progressive agendas, elect progressive candidates, and steer the Democratic Party ever-further towards the Left.

"The Islamophobia Misinformation Experts"

Then comes chapter two, on the five men "primarily responsible for orchestrating the majority of anti-Islam messages polluting our national discourse today," already identified above as Frank Gaffney, David Yerushalmi, Daniel Pipes, Robert Spencer and Steven Emerson.

These men are "intentionally misdefining" Sharia as "a totalitarian ideology" "for their own monetary and political ends," the report claims. Its authors say that Sharia, or Islamic religious law, is observed "in part and in different ways by every practicing Muslim." The authors then put forward that the above "misinformation experts" "are effectively arguing that only the extremists' interpretations of Islam are authentic, and that therefore the diversity of moderate interpretations within Islam is meaningless."

As Spencer puts it on his website, Jihad Watch,

Because Sharia originates with the Quran and the Sunnah [the teachings and precedents of Muhammad], it is not optional. Sharia is the legal code ordained by Allah for all mankind. To violate Sharia or not to accept its authority is to commit rebellion against Allah, which Allah's faithful are required to combat . . .

[T]here are few aspects of life that Sharia does not specifically govern. Everything from washing one's hands to child-rearing to taxation to military policy fall under its dictates. Because Sharia is derivate of the Quran and the Sunnah, it affords some room for interpretation. But upon examination of the Islamic sources . . . it is apparent that any meaningful application of Sharia is going to look very different from anything resembling a free or open society in the Western sense. The stoning of adulterers, execution of apostates and blasphemers, repression of other religions, and a mandatory hostility toward non-Islamic nations punctuated by regular warfare will be the norm. It seems fair then to classify Islam and its Sharia code as a form of totalitarianism.

All Islamic scholars agree that Sharia embraces the law, the state, religion and politics.

But don't take Spencer's word for it. Instead, rely on the authoritative opinion of Sheikh Yusuf al-Qaradawi, who, as Joseph Klein writes,

> is listed as fourteenth out of 500 of the world's influential Muslim figures, according to the most recent study released by the Royal Islamic Strategic Studies Center and the Prince Al-Waleed Bin Talal Center for Muslim-Christian Understanding at Georgetown University . . .

Qaradawi, the spiritual leader of the Muslim Brotherhood, was one of the scholars who endorsed the 2004 "Amman Message," a document the CAP authors rely on to show what they called "the dynamic, interpretive tradition of Islam in practice."

Does Qaradawi agree with the CAP authors' description of Sharia as "not political" and "in harmony with the core values at the heart of America"? Not a chance. As he explains in his book, *"Al-Din wal-Siyasa"* (*Religion and Politics*), all Islamic scholars agree that Sharia embraces the law, the state, religion and politics:

The Islamic shari'ah governs all of the actions of those who are obligated (to it). There is no act or occurrence which exists without a corresponding ruling from one of the five shari'ah rulings (obligatory, recommended, prohibited, reprehensible, or permitted). This has been confirmed by fundamentalists and scholars from every faction and school of thought associated with Islam ... Whoever reads the books of the Islamic shari'ah, I mean the books of Islamic jurisprudence, in its different schools of thought, will find that they comprise all of the affairs of life, from the jurisprudence of purity, to that of the family, society, and the state. This is very clear for every elementary student, not to mention those in the world who are more capable.

Moreover, Qaradawi said that Sharia is not a pick-and-choose menu, as CAP's authors would have us believe. Islam "rejects the partitioning of its rulings and teachings," he declared. Nor is Sharia an ever evolving religious guidepost for human behavior, subject to change by human beings. "Shariah cannot be amended to conform to changing human values and standards," said Qaradawi ...

In sum, Qaradawi's description of Sharia sounds much closer to the way that Frank Gaffney's Center for Security Policy, one of CAP's targets for condemnation, has described Sharia in its book *"Sharia: The Threat To America"*:

[A] "complete way of life" (social, cultural, military, religious, and political), governed from cradle to grave by Islamic law ... Shariah is, moreover, a doctrine that mandates the rule of Allah over all aspects of society. . . .

The Validators

The report labels some lesser-known experts about radical Islam as "validators" who help "authenticate manufactured myths about Muslims and Islam." As with the five primary "Islamophobes," the report devotes virtually no space to refuting the substance of the validators' so-called "manufactured myths"; instead, these figures are simply painted as anti-Muslim bigots. . . .

"The Right-Wing Media Enablers"

Chapter four takes on two prominent figures who serve, according to the report, as bullhorns for the anti-Islam propaganda espoused by the aforementioned "Islamophobes": David Horowitz and his Freedom Center organization, with its websites *FrontPage Magazine* and Jihad Watch, and Pamela Geller's blog, "Atlas Shrugs."

As with so many of the accusations in "Fear Inc.," the report cites selective, incomplete quotes from Horowitz and Geller, often out of context, and sources them sometimes to "dead" web links in the footnotes or to such leftist sources as the Southern Poverty Law Center (SPLC), which is hilariously described as "nonpartisan."

An SPLC report calls the David Horowitz Freedom Center one of the main organizations that "helped spread bigoted ideas into American life." Among these so-called bigoted ideas that the SPLC report notes are the historical truths that Africans, abetted by Arabs, contributed to the slave trade, and that "there never was an anti-slavery movement until white Christians created one." To disprove this latter quote from Horowitz, the SPLC report mentions historical slave revolts, such as the famous one of Spartacus against Rome, as evidence to the contrary. *Of course* there were slave revolts—but a revolt of slaves themselves is not the same as an anti-slavery movement among non-slaves. . . .

As for Pamela Geller, some of the report's criticism of her is guilt-by-association with other "Islamophobes" like Gaffney, Yerushalmi, and—you guessed it, Breivik, who cited her twelve times in his manifesto CAP wants you to know. The report also notes that she is "best known as the public face of the protest against" what it innocuously refers to as "the Park51 community center in lower New York City."

"Fear, Inc." consists precisely of what it accuses its targets of—slanderous fear-mongering.

Additionally, it attacks her for such "outrageous and racist claims" as suggesting that [Barack] Obama was "essentially backing Al Qaeda in Libya"—which he did, by supplying al Qaeda-backed rebels there with arms and support—and saying that "everything this president has done so far has helped foster America's submission to Islam"—which he has. She is charged further with "conspiratorial claims" that include:

President Obama is a Muslim; Arabic is not just a language but actually a spearhead for anti-Americanism; radical Islam has infiltrated our government, which is being run by Islamic supremacists; and Muslims are engaged in stealth cultural jihad by wearing their headscarves at Disneyland . . .

Geller also sees the enemy Islam infiltrating President Obama's administration. Beyond that, Geller is convinced that President Obama has been, or continues to be, a practicing Muslim. Geller says President Obama is a "muhammadan" who "wants jihad to win."

Bold positions? Yes—Geller has a take-no-prisoners style. But that doesn't make her Islamophobic *or* wrong. As with most of the other "Islamophobic" claims noted in "Fear, Inc.", the report does not present her arguments for her positions, much less refute them, either because the authors of the report cannot or because it is easier and a more effective strategy to simply cite them as *prima facie* evidence of Islamophobia.

The Threat Comes from Islamist Supremacists, Not Islamophobia

"Fear, Inc." consists precisely of what it accuses its targets of—slanderous fear-mongering. The report, like the very concept of "Islamophobia," is a bludgeon to silence the critics of radical Islam, who they claim "spread a deliberately misleading message about Islam and Muslims that is fundamentally antithetical to our nation's founding principles of religious freedom, inclusivity, and pluralism." On the contrary, it is precisely in defense of those principles that the so-called "Islamophobes" in question literally risk their lives to expose and confront the threat of Islamic fundamentalism.

At the close of the report's introduction, the authors make this proclamation:

> It is our view that in order to safeguard our national security and uphold America's core values, we must return to a fact-based civil discourse regarding the challenges we face as a nation and world. This discourse must be frank and honest, but also consistent with American values of religious liberty, equal justice under the law, and respect for pluralism.

Bravo. No disagreement there. Indeed, it *is* a matter of national security that we return to a fact-based, frank and honest civil discourse about the current challenges to American values, including the subversive threat of the Muslim Brotherhood's influence on our shores. But the authors say only that this threat has been entirely manufactured by Islamophobic bigots. They go on to say that

> [a] first step toward the goal of honest, civil discourse is to expose—and marginalize—the influence of the individuals and groups who make up the Islamophobia network in America by actively working to divide Americans against one another through misinformation.

Replace the fanciful phrase "Islamophobia network" in that paragraph with "Islamic supremacists and their supporters," and we will have made a very significant first step indeed.

Islamophobia Is a Bigger Threat than Islam

Melody Moezzi

Melody Moezzi is an Iranian-American Muslim writer and at-torney who has written for The Washington Post, The Huffing-ton Post, *and* Ms. Magazine, *among other publications. She is the author of* War on Error: Real Stories of American Muslims *and is the executive director of the Atlanta-based interfaith non-profit, 100 People of Faith.*

When you hear the word "terrorist," who comes to mind? Basque separatists in white hoods? Anarchists wearing bandanas with five-pointed stars? Or perhaps some right- or left-wing pariah building bombs in basements?

Westerners Feel Threatened by Muslims

My guess is that none of these characters wins top billing in the minds of most people when they think of terrorists. Why? Mainly because we don't generally hear about these kinds of terrorists in the news, and when we do, they aren't typically called "terrorists." They're called murderers, thugs or lunatics. These days, when we read or hear the term "terrorist" in the news, it's almost always accompanied by some reference to "Islamic extremism" or worse yet, to Islam itself.

So, it must be that most terrorists are in fact Islamists, right? Not so much.

According to the 2010 *EU Terrorism Situation and Trend Report*, "294 failed, foiled, or successfully executed attacks" oc-curred in 2009, in six European countries—down almost 50 percent from 2007. The breakdown of attacks with respect to responsibility was thus: 237 by separatist groups; 40 by left-wing and anarchist groups; four by rightists; ten with no clear affiliation; two by single-issue groups, and one by so-called Islamists.

And yet, the report points out: "Islamist terrorism is still perceived as the biggest threat to most Member States, despite the fact that only one Islamist terrorist attack—a bomb attack in Italy—took place in the EU [European Union] in 2009."

So, why is this? Why is it that according to a poll of 1,600 French and German citizens recently published in *Le Monde*, 40 percent of them consider Islam a threat? Why is it that the Swiss felt compelled to outlaw minarets? Why is it that so many Americans are up in arms about the building of an Islamic community center in downtown Manhattan?

Clearly, many people—particularly in Europe and the U.S.—feel threatened by the amorphous group of over a billion people worldwide known collectively as "Muslims."

Islamophobia is far more threatening than any Muslim could ever be, for it breeds ignorance and bigotry.

As a member of this collective, I have a few things to say to those who feel threatened by me and my kind:

First, it's not your fault. Members of the media, including myself, need to start choosing our words more carefully. If individuals within any given community employ violence against a particular group or nation in an effort to evoke widespread fear and panic, then those individuals are terrorists. Period. Their religion is irrelevant. Even if they claim to be murdering an abortionist in service to Christianity or an Israeli in service to Islam or a Palestinian in service to Judaism, they are not legitimate representatives of any of the faiths they claim to be following and they, in fact, do them all a disservice.

Secondly, your fear is irrational. Look at the statistics above; go meet your Muslim neighbors, and get over it.

Lastly, and perhaps most importantly, your fears are counterproductive. Islamophobia is far more threatening than any Muslim could ever be, for it breeds ignorance and bigotry. It also only further alienates Muslims, and if you've ever been alienated or outcast, you know how vulnerable it makes you to radicalization. It's why people join gangs; it's why people form crappy garage bands, and it's why people become terrorists. Nothing is more threatening than hating and fearing another person for no good reason.

An Irrational Fear of Islam Has Its Roots in the Time of the Crusades

John Feffer

John Feffer is the codirector of Foreign Policy in Focus at the Institute for Policy Studies and writes the institute's regular "World Beat" column. He is the author of Crusade 2.0: The West's Resurgent War on Islam.

The Muslims were bloodthirsty and treacherous. They conducted a sneak attack against the French army and slaughtered every single soldier, 20,000 in all. More than 1,000 years ago, in the mountain passes of Spain, the Muslim horde cut down the finest soldiers in Charlemagne's command, including his brave nephew Roland. Then, according to the famous poem that immortalized the tragedy, Charlemagne exacted his revenge by routing the entire Muslim army.

The Crusades Began an Image Problem for Muslims

The *Song of Roland*, an eleventh century rendering in verse of an eighth century battle, is a staple of Western Civilization classes at colleges around the country. A "masterpiece of epic drama," in the words of its renowned translator Dorothy Sayers, it provides a handy preface for students before they delve into readings on the Crusades that began in 1095. More ominously, the poem has schooled generations of Judeo-Christians to view Muslims as perfidious enemies who once threatened the very foundations of Western civilization.

John Feffer, "The Lies of Islamophobia: The Three Unfinished Wars of the West Against the Rest," TomDispatch.com, November 7, 2010. Copyright © 2010 by John Feffer. All rights reserved. Reproduced by permission.

The problem, however, is that the whole epic is built on a curious falsehood. The army that fell upon Roland and his Frankish soldiers was not Muslim at all. In the real battle of 778, the slayers of the Franks were Christian Basques furious at Charlemagne for pillaging their city of Pamplona. Not epic at all, the battle emerged from a parochial dispute in the complex wars of medieval Spain. Only later, as kings and popes and knights prepared to do battle in the First Crusade, did an anonymous bard repurpose the text to serve the needs of an emerging cross-against-crescent holy war.

Similarly, we think of the Crusades as the archetypal "clash of civilizations" between the followers of Jesus and the followers of Mohammed. In the popular version of those Crusades, the Muslim adversary has, in fact, replaced a remarkable range of peoples the Crusaders dealt with as enemies, including Jews killed in pogroms on the way to the Holy Land, rival Catholics slaughtered in the Balkans and in Constantinople, and Christian heretics hunted down in southern France.

What really keeps Islamophobes up at night is . . . the growing economic, political, and global influence of modern, mainstream Islam.

Much later, during the Cold War, mythmakers in Washington performed a similar act, substituting a monolithic crew labeled "godless communists" for a disparate group of anti-imperial nationalists in an attempt to transform conflicts in remote locations like Vietnam, Guatemala, and Iran into epic struggles between the forces of the Free World and the forces of evil. In recent years, the [George W.] Bush administration did it all over again by portraying Arab nationalists as fiendish Islamic fundamentalists when we invaded Iraq and prepared to topple the regime in Syria.

The Crusades Continue to Shape Opinion

Similar mythmaking continues today. The recent surge of Islamophobia in the United States has drawn strength from several extraordinary substitutions. A clearly Christian president has become Muslim in the minds of a significant number of Americans. The thoughtful Islamic scholar Tariq Ramadan has become a closet fundamentalist in the writings of Paul Berman and others. And an Islamic center in lower Manhattan, organized by proponents of interfaith dialogue, has become an extremist "mosque at Ground Zero" in the TV appearances, political speeches, and Internet sputterings of a determined clique of right-wing activists.

This transformation of Islam into a violent caricature of itself—as if [conservative political commentator] Ann Coulter had suddenly morphed into the face of Christianity—comes at a somewhat strange juncture in the United States. Anti-Islamic rhetoric and hate crimes, which spiked immediately after September 11, 2001, had been on the wane. No major terrorist attack had taken place in the U.S. or Europe since the London bombings in 2005. The current American president [Barack Obama] had reached out to the Muslim world and retired the controversial acronym GWOT, or "Global War on Terror."

All the elements seemed in place, in other words, for us to turn the page on an ugly chapter in our history. Yet it's as if we remain fixed in the eleventh century in a perpetual battle of "us" against "them." Like the undead rising from their coffins, our previous "crusades" never go away. Indeed, we still seem to be fighting the three great wars of the millennium, even though two of these conflicts have long been over and the third has been rhetorically reduced to "overseas contingency operations." The Crusades, which finally petered out in the seventeenth century, continue to shape our global imagination today. The Cold War ended in 1991, but key elements of the anti-communism credo have been awkwardly grafted onto the new Islamist adversary. And the Global War on Terror, which President Obama quietly renamed shortly after taking office, has in fact metastasized into the wars that his administration continues to prosecute in Afghanistan, Pakistan, Iraq, Yemen, and elsewhere.

Those in Europe and the United States who cheer on these wars claim that they are issuing a wake-up call about the continued threat of al-Qaeda, the Taliban, and other militants who claim the banner of Islam. However, what really keeps Islamophobes up at night is not the marginal and backwards-looking Islamic fundamentalists but rather the growing economic, political, and global influence of modern, mainstream Islam. Examples of Islam successfully grappling with modernity abound, from Turkey's new foreign policy and Indonesia's economic muscle to the Islamic political parties participating in elections in Lebanon, Morocco, and Jordan. Instead of providing reassurance, however, these trends only incite Islamophobes to intensify their battles to "save" Western civilization.

As long as our unfinished wars still burn in the collective consciousness—and still rage in Kabul, Baghdad, Sana'a, and the Tribal Areas of Pakistan—Islamophobia will make its impact felt in our media, politics, and daily life. Only if we decisively end the millennial Crusades, the half-century Cold War, and the decade-long War on Terror (under whatever name) will we overcome the dangerous divide that has consumed so many lives, wasted so much wealth, and distorted our very understanding of our Western selves.

Islamophobia Is Irrational

With their irrational fear of spiders, arachnophobes are scared of both harmless daddy longlegs and poisonous brown recluse spiders. In extreme cases, an arachnophobe can break out in a sweat while merely looking at photos of spiders. It is, of course, reasonable to steer clear of black widows. What makes a legitimate fear into an irrational phobia, however, is the tendency to lump all of any group, spiders or humans, into one lethal category and then to exaggerate how threatening they are. Spider bites, after all, are responsible for at most a handful of deaths a year in the United States.

The myth of Islam as a "religion of the sword" was a staple of Crusader literature and art.

Islamophobia is, similarly, an irrational fear of Islam. Yes, certain Muslim fundamentalists have been responsible for terrorist attacks, certain fantasists about a "global caliphate" continue to plot attacks on perceived enemies, and certain groups like Afghanistan's Taliban and Somalia's al-Shabaab practice medieval versions of the religion. But Islamophobes confuse these small parts with the whole and then see terrorist *jihad* [holy war] under every Islamic pillow. They break out in a sweat at the mere picture of an *imam* [Muslim prayer leader].

Irrational fears are often rooted in our dimly remembered childhoods. Our irrational fear of Islam similarly seems to stem from events that happened in the early days of Christendom. Three myths inherited from the era of the Crusades constitute the core of Islamophobia today: Muslims are inherently violent, Muslims want to take over the world, and Muslims can't be trusted.

The myth of Islam as a "religion of the sword" was a staple of Crusader literature and art. In fact, the atrocities committed by Muslim leaders and armies—and there were some— rarely rivaled the slaughters of the Crusaders, who retook Jerusalem in 1099 in a veritable bloodbath. "The heaps of the dead presented an immediate problem for the conquerors," writes Christopher Tyerman in *God's War*. "Many of the surviving Muslim population were forced to clear the streets and carry the bodies outside the walls to be burnt in great pyres, whereat they themselves were massacred." Jerusalem's Jews suffered a similar fate when the Crusaders burned many of them alive in their main synagogue. Four hundred years earlier, by contrast, Caliph 'Umar put no one to the sword when he took over Jerusalem, signing a pact with the Christian patriarch Sophronius that pledged "no compulsion in religion."

This myth of the inherently violent Muslim endures. Islam "teaches violence," televangelist Pat Robertson proclaimed in 2005. "The Koran teaches violence and most Muslims, including so-called moderate Muslims, openly believe in violence," was the way Major General Jerry Curry (U.S. Army, ret.), who served in the [Jimmy] Carter, [Ronald] Reagan, and [George] Bush Sr. administrations, put it.

The Crusaders justified their violence by arguing that Muslims were bent on taking over the world. In its early days, the expanding Islamic empire did indeed imagine an ever-growing *dar-es-Islam* (House of Islam). By the time of the Crusades, however, this initial burst of enthusiasm for holy war had long been spent. Moreover, the Christian West harbored its own set of desires when it came to extending the Pope's authority to every corner of the globe. Even that early believer in soft power, Francis of Assisi, sat down with Sultan al-Kamil during the Fifth Crusade with the aim of eliminating Islam through conversion.

Today, Islamophobes portray the building of Cordoba House in lower Manhattan as just another gambit in this millennial power grab: "This is Islamic domination and expansionism," writes right-wing blogger Pamela Geller, who made the "Ground Zero Mosque" into a media obsession. "Islam is a religion with a very political agenda," warns ex-Muslim Ali Sina. "The ultimate goal of Islam is to rule the world."

These two myths—of inherent violence and global ambitions—led to the firm conviction that Muslims were by nature untrustworthy. . . .

For Islamophobes today, Muslims abroad are similarly terrorists-in-waiting. As for Muslims at home, "American Muslims must face their either/or," writes the novelist Edward

Cline, "to repudiate Islam or remain a quiet, sanctioning fifth column." Even American Muslims in high places, like Congressman Keith Ellison (D-MN), are not above suspicion. In a 2006 CNN interview, [host] Glenn Beck said, "I have been nervous about this interview with you, because what I feel like saying is, 'Sir, prove to me that you are not working with our enemies.'"

In 1951, the CIA and the emerging anti-communist elite . . . created the Crusade for Freedom . . . against the Soviet Union.

These three myths of Islamophobia flourish in our era, just as they did almost a millennium ago, because of a cunning conflation of a certain type of Islamic fundamentalism with Islam itself. [Political commentator] Bill O'Reilly was neatly channeling this Crusader mindset when he asserted recently that "the Muslim threat to the world is not isolated. It's huge!" When Deputy Undersecretary of Defense for Intelligence William Boykin, in an infamous 2003 sermon, thundered "What I'm here to do today is to recruit you to be warriors of God's kingdom," he was issuing the Crusader call to arms.

But O'Reilly and Boykin, who represent the violence, duplicity, and expansionist mind-set of today's Western crusaders, were also invoking a more recent tradition, closer in time and far more familiar.

The Totalitarian Myth

In 1951, the CIA and the emerging anti-communist elite, including soon-to-be-president Dwight Eisenhower, created the Crusade for Freedom as a key component of a growing psychological warfare campaign against the Soviet Union and the satellite countries it controlled in Eastern Europe. The language of this "crusade" was intentionally religious. It reached out to "peoples deeply rooted in the heritage of western civilization," living under the "crushing weight of a godless dictatorship." In its call for the liberation of the communist world, it echoed the nearly thousand-year-old crusader rhetoric of "recovering" Jerusalem and other outposts of Christianity.

In the theology of the Cold War, the Soviet Union replaced the Islamic world as the untrustworthy infidel. However unconsciously, the old crusader myths about Islam translated remarkably easily into governing assumptions about the communist enemy: the Soviets and their allies were bent on taking over the world, could not be trusted with their rhetoric of peaceful coexistence, imperiled Western civilization, and fought with unique savagery as well as a willingness to martyr themselves for the greater ideological good.

Ironically, Western governments were so obsessed with fighting this new scourge that, in the Cold War years, on the theory that my enemy's enemy is my friend, they nurtured radical Islam as a weapon. As journalist Robert Dreyfuss ably details in his book *The Devil's Game*, the U.S. funding of the *mujahideen* [Muslim guerilla fighters who battled the Soviets] in Afghanistan was only one part of the anti-communist crusade in the Islamic world. To undermine Arab nationalists and leftists who might align themselves with the Soviet Union, the United States (and Israel) worked with Iranian mullahs [religious teachers], helped create Hamas [terrorist organization], and facilitated the spread of the Muslim Brotherhood.

Though the Cold War ended with the sudden disappearance of the Soviet Union in 1991, that era's mind-set—and so many of the Cold Warriors sporting it—never went with it. The prevailing mythology was simply transferred back to the Islamic world. In anti-communist theology, for example, the worst curse word was "totalitarianism," said to describe the essence of the all-encompassing Soviet state and system. According to the gloss that early neoconservative Jeanne Kirkpatrick provided in her book *Dictatorships and Double Standards*, the

West had every reason to support right-wing authoritarian dictatorships because they would steadfastly oppose left-wing totalitarian dictatorships, which, unlike the autocracies we allied with, were supposedly incapable of internal reform.

According to the new "Islamo-fascism" school—and its acolytes like Norman Podhoretz, David Horowitz, Bill O'Reilly, Pamela Geller—the fundamentalists are simply the "new totalitarians," as hidebound, fanatical, and incapable of change as communists. For a more sophisticated treatment of the Islamo-fascist argument, check out Paul Berman, a rightward-leaning liberal intellectual who has tried to demonstrate that "moderate Muslims" are fundamentalists in reformist clothing.

These Cold Warriors all treat the Islamic world as an undifferentiated mass—in spirit, a modern Soviet Union—where Arab governments and radical Islamists work hand in glove. They simply fail to grasp that the Syrian, Egyptian, and Saudi Arabian governments have launched their own attacks on radical Islam. The sharp divides between the Iranian regime and the Taliban, between the Jordanian government and the Palestinians, between Shi'ites and Sunni in Iraq, and even among Kurds all disappear in the totalitarian blender, just as anti-communists generally failed to distinguish between the Communist hardliner Leonid Brezhnev and the Communist reformer Mikhail Gorbachev.

"Since the early 1990s, 23 Muslim countries have developed more democratic institutions."

At the root of terrorism, according to Berman, are "immense failures of political courage and imagination within the Muslim world," rather than the violent fantasies of a group of religious outliers or the Crusader-ish military operations of the West. In other words, something flawed at the very core of

Islam itself is responsible for the violence done in its name—a line of argument remarkably similar to one Cold Warriors made about communism.

All of this, of course, represents a mirror image of al-Qaeda's arguments about the inherent perversities of the infidel West. As during the Cold War, hardliners reinforce one another.

The persistence of Crusader myths and their transposition into a Cold War framework help explain why the West is saddled with so many misconceptions about Islam. They don't, however, explain the recent spike in Islamophobia in the U.S. after several years of relative tolerance. . . .

Fanning the Flames

[Nine] years after September 11th [2001] a second spike in Islamophobia *and* in home-grown terrorist attacks like that of the would-be Times Square bomber has been born of two intersecting pressures: American critics of Obama's foreign policy believe that he has backed away from the major civilizational struggle of our time, even as many in the Muslim world see Obama-era foreign policy as a continuation, even an escalation, of Bush-era policies of war and occupation.

Here is the irony: alongside the indisputable rise of fundamentalism over the last two decades, only some of it oriented towards violence, the Islamic world has undergone a shift which deep-sixes the cliché that Islam has held countries back from political and economic development. "Since the early 1990s, 23 Muslim countries have developed more democratic institutions, with fairly run elections, energized and competitive political parties, greater civil liberties, or better legal protections for journalists," writes Philip Howard in *The Digital Origins of Dictatorship and Democracy*. Turkey has emerged as a vibrant democracy and a major foreign policy player. Indonesia, the world's most populous Muslim country, is now the largest economy in Southeast Asia and the eighteenth largest economy in the world.

Are Islamophobes missing this story of mainstream Islam's accommodation with democracy and economic growth? Or is it this story (not Islamo-fascism starring al-Qaeda) that is their real concern?

The recent preoccupations of Islamophobes are telling in this regard. Pamela Geller, after all, was typical in the way she went after not a radical mosque, but an Islamic center about two blocks from Ground Zero proposed by a proponent of interfaith dialogue. As journalist Stephen Salisbury writes, "The mosque controversy is not really about a mosque at all; it's about the presence of Muslims in America, and the free-floating anxiety and fear that now dominate the nation's psyche." For her latest venture, Geller is pushing a boycott of Campbell's Soup because it accepts *halal* certification—the Islamic version of kosher certification by a rabbi—from the Islamic Society of North America, a group which, by the way, has gone out of its way to denounce religious extremism.

Paul Berman, meanwhile, has devoted his latest book, *The Flight of the Intellectuals*, to deconstructing the arguments not of Osama bin-Laden or his ilk, but of Tariq Ramadan, the foremost mainstream Islamic theologian. Ramadan is a man firmly committed to breaking down the old distinctions between "us" and "them." Critical of the West for colonialism, racism, and other ills, he also challenges the injustices of the Islamic world. He is far from a fundamentalist.

And what country, by the way, has exercised European Islamophobes more than any other? Pakistan? Saudi Arabia? Taliban Afghanistan? No, the answer is: Turkey. "The Turks are conquering Germany in the same way the Kosovars conquered Kosovo: by using higher birthrates," argues Germany's Islamophobe *du jour*, Thilo Sarrazin, a member of Germany's Social

Democratic Party. The far right has even united around a Europe-wide referendum to keep Turkey out of the European Union.

Despite his many defects, George W. Bush at least knew enough to distinguish Islam from Islamism. By targeting a perfectly normal Islamic center, a perfectly normal Islamic scholar, and a perfectly normal Islamic country—all firmly in the mainstream of that religion—the Islamophobes have actually declared war on normalcy, not extremism.

The victories of the tea party movement and the increased power of Republican militants in Congress, not to mention the renaissance of the far right in Europe, suggest that we will be living with this Islamophobia and the three unfinished wars of the West against the Rest for some time. The Crusades lasted hundreds of years. Let's hope that Crusade 2.0, and the dark age that we find ourselves in, has a far shorter lifespan.

CHAPTER 4

Does Sharia Law Pose a Threat to America?

Overview: Background on Sharia Law

Toni Johnson

Toni Johnson is a senior staff writer for the Council on Foreign Relations.

Sharia, or Islamic law, influences the legal code in most Muslim countries. A movement to allow sharia to govern personal status law, a set of regulations that pertain to marriage, divorce, inheritance, and custody, is even expanding into the West. "There are so many varying interpretations of what sharia actually means that in some places it can be incorporated into political systems relatively easily," says Steven A. Cook, CFR [Council on Foreign Relations] senior fellow for Middle Eastern studies. Sharia's influence on both personal status law and criminal law is highly controversial, though. Some interpretations are used to justify cruel punishments such as amputation and stoning as well as unequal treatment of women in inheritance, dress, and independence. The debate is growing as to whether sharia can coexist with secularism, democracy, or even modernity.

What Is Sharia?

Also meaning "path" in Arabic, sharia guides all aspects of Muslim life including daily routines, familial and religious obligations, and financial dealings. It is derived primarily from the Quran and the Sunna—the sayings, practices, and teachings of the Prophet Mohammed. Precedents and analogy applied by Muslim scholars are used to address new issues. The consensus of the Muslim community also plays a role in defining this theological manual.

Sharia developed several hundred years after the Prophet Mohammed's death in 632 CE [Common Era] as the Islamic empire expanded to the edge of North Africa in the West and to China in the East. Since the Prophet Mohammed was considered the most pious of all believers, his life and ways became a model for all other Muslims and were collected by scholars into what is known as the *hadith*. As each locality tried to reconcile local customs and Islam, *hadith* literature grew and developed into distinct schools of Islamic thought: the Sunni schools, Hanbali, Maliki, Shafi'i, Hanafi; and the Shiite school, Ja'fari. Named after the scholars that inspired them, they differ in the weight each applies to the sources from which sharia is derived, the Quran, *hadith*, Islamic scholars, and consensus of the community. . . .

Controversy: Punishment and Equality Under Sharia

Marriage and divorce are the most significant aspects of sharia, but criminal law is the most controversial. In sharia, there are categories of offenses: those that are prescribed a specific punishment in the Quran, known as *hadd* punishments, those that fall under a judge's discretion, and those resolved through a tit-for-tat measure (i.e., blood money paid to the family of a murder victim). There are five *hadd* crimes: unlawful sexual intercourse (sex outside of marriage and adultery), false accusation of unlawful sexual intercourse, wine drinking (sometimes extended to include all alcohol drinking), theft, and highway robbery. Punishments for *hadd* offenses—flogging, stoning, amputation, exile, or execution—get a significant amount of media attention when they occur. These sentences are not often prescribed, however. "In reality, most Muslim countries do not use traditional classical Islamic punishments," says Ali Mazrui of the Institute of Global Cultural Studies in a Voice of America interview. These punishments remain on the books in some countries but lesser penalties are often considered sufficient.

Despite official reluctance to use *hadd* punishments, vigilante justice still takes place. Honor killings, murders committed in retaliation for bringing dishonor on one's family, are a worldwide problem. While precise statistics are scarce, the UN [United Nations] estimates thousands of women are killed annually in the name of family honor. Other practices that are woven into the sharia debate, such as female genital mutilation, adolescent marriages, polygamy, and gender-biased inheritance rules, elicit as much controversy. There is significant debate over what the Quran sanctions and what practices were pulled from local customs and predate Islam. Those that seek to eliminate or at least modify these controversial practices cite the religious tenet of *tajdid*. The concept is one of renewal, where Islamic society must be reformed constantly to keep it in its purest form. "With the passage of time and changing circumstances since traditional classical jurisprudence was founded, people's problems have changed and conversely, there must be new thought to address these changes and events," says Dr. Abdul Fatah Idris, head of the comparative jurisprudence department at Al-Azhar University in Cairo. Though many scholars share this line of thought, there are those who consider the purest form of Islam to be the one practiced in the seventh century.

Some Muslim scholars say that secular government is the best way to observe sharia.

Sharia Versus Secularism

The issue of sharia law versus secular law gained new scrutiny in 2011 in the wake of uprisings in several Arab countries, such as Libya, Tunisia, and Egypt, which ousted pro-Western autocrats and helped Islamist political parties gain prominence. A 2010 Pew poll conducted in seven countries including Egypt found strong support for Islam in politics and for harsh punishments for crimes such as theft, adultery, and conversion away from Islam. At the same time, a majority of those polled in every country except Pakistan believed democracy is the best form of governance. Whether democracy and Islam can coexist is a topic of heated debate. Some Islamists argue democracy is a purely Western concept imposed on Muslim countries. Others feel Islam necessitates a democratic system and that democracy has a basis in the Quran since "mutual consultation" among the people is commended. . . .

Noah Feldman, a former CFR adjunct senior fellow, wrote in a 2008 *New York Times Magazine* article that the full incorporation of Islamic law is viewed as creating "a path to just and legitimate government in much of the Muslim world." It places duplicitous rulers alongside their constituents under the rule of Cod. "For many Muslims today, living in corrupt autocracies, the call for [sharia] is not a call for sexism, obscurantism or savage punishment but for an Islamic version of what the West considers its most prized principle of political justice: the rule of law," Feldman argues.

On the other hand, some Muslim scholars say that secular government is the best way to observe sharia. "Enforcing a [sharia] through coercive power of the state negates its religious nature, because Muslims would be observing the law of the state and not freely performing their religious obligation as Muslims," says Abdullahi Ahmed An-Na'im, a professor of law at Emory University and author of a book on the future of sharia. Opinions on the best balance of Islamic law and secular law vary, but sharia has been incorporated into political systems in three general ways:

- *Dual Legal System.* Many majority Muslim countries
  have a dual system in which the government is secular
  but Muslims can choose to bring familial and financial
  disputes to sharia courts. The exact jurisdiction of these
  courts varies from country to country, but usually includes marriage, divorce, inheritance, and guardianship.

Examples can be seen in Nigeria and Kenya, which have sharia courts that rule on family law for Muslims. A variation exists in Tanzania, where civil courts apply sharia or secular law according to the religious backgrounds of the defendants. Several countries, including Lebanon and Indonesia, have mixed jurisdiction courts based on residual colonial legal systems and supplemented with sharia. Western countries are also exploring the idea of allowing Muslims to apply Islamic law in familial and financial disputes. In late 2008, Britain officially allowed sharia tribunals (*NYT*) governing marriage, divorce, and inheritance to make legally binding decisions if both parties agreed. The new system is in line with separate mediation allowed for Anglican and Jewish communities in England. Criminal law remains under the gavel of the existing legal system. "There is no reason why principles of sharia law, or any other religious code, should not be the basis for mediation," Britain's top judge, Lord Nicholas Phillips, said in a July 2008 speech. Supporters of this initiative, such as the archbishop of Canterbury, Rowan Williams, argue that it would help maintain social cohesion in European societies increasingly divided by religion. However, some research suggests the process to be discriminatory toward women. Other analysts suggest the system has led to grey areas. Britain's Muslims come from all over the world, Ishtiaq Ahmed, a spokesperson for the Council for Mosques in England, told the BBC, noting that this makes it hard to discern at times "where the rulings of the sharia finish and long-held cultural practices start." Sharia has recently become a topic of political concern in the United States. The state of Oklahoma passed a ballot measure in November 2010 to ban the use of sharia law in court cases, which supporters are calling "a preemptive strike against Islamic law." Several opponents of new mosques being built around the United States, including one near Ground Zero, have cited fear of the spread of sharia as a reason for opposition. And about a third of Americans in an August 2010 *Newsweek* poll suspect U.S. President Barack Obama sympathizes with Islamist goals to impose sharia.

- *Government under God.* In those Muslim countries where Islam is the official religion listed in the constitution, sharia is declared to be a source, or the source, of the laws. Examples include Saudi Arabia, Kuwait, Bahrain, Yemen, and the United Arab Emirates, where the governments derive their legitimacy from Islam. In Pakistan, Egypt, Iran, and Iraq, among others, it is also forbidden to enact legislation that is antithetical to Islam. Saudi Arabia employs one of the strictest interpretations of sharia. Women are not allowed to drive, are under the guardianship of male relatives at all times, and must be completely covered in public. Elsewhere, governments are much more lenient, as in the United Arab Emirates, where alcohol is tolerated. Non-Muslims are not expected to obey sharia and in most countries, they are the jurisdiction of special committees and adjunct courts under the control of the government.

- *Completely Secular.* Muslim countries where the government is declared to be secular in the constitution include Azerbaijan, Tajikistan, Chad, Somalia, and Senegal. Islamist parties run for office occasionally in these countries and sharia often influences local customs. Popular Islamist groups are often viewed as a threat by existing governments. As in Azerbaijan in the 1990s, secularism is sometimes upheld by severe government crackdowns on Islamist groups and political parties. Similar clashes have occurred in Turkey. Under the suspicion that the majority party, the Islamist Justice and Development Party, was trying to establish sharia, Turkey's chief prosecutor petitioned the constitutional court in March 2008 to bar the party from politics altogether. One of the politicians indicted, Prime Minister Recep Tayyip Erdogan, told *Newsweek*, "Turkey has achieved what people said could never be achieved—a balance between Islam, democracy, secularism and modernity." Secular Muslim countries are a minority, however, and the popularity of Islamist political parties are narrowing the gap between religion and state.

There Is a Link Between Sharia Law and the Support of Violent Jihad

Mordechai Kedar and David Yerushalmi

Mordechai Kedar is an assistant professor in the departments of Arabic and Middle East studies and a research associate with the Begin-Sadat (BESA) Center for Strategic Studies, both at Bar-Ilan University in Israel. David Yerushalmi is general counsel for the Center for Security Policy and director of policy studies at the Institute for Advanced Strategic and Political Studies.

How great is the danger of extremist violence in the name of Islam in the United States? Recent congressional hearings [held in March 2011] into this question by Rep. Peter King (Republican of New York), chairman of the Committee on Homeland Security, have generated a firestorm of controversy among his colleagues, the press, and the general public. Though similar hearings have taken place at least fourteen times since 2001, King was labeled a latter-day Joe McCarthy [senator who conducted anti-communist hearings in the 1950s] and the hearings called an assault on civil liberties and a contemporary witch-hunt. Yet the larger dilemmas outlined by both the congressman and some of his witnesses remain: To what extent are American Muslims, native-born as well as naturalized, being radicalized by Islamists? And what steps can those who are sworn to the protection of American citizenry take that will uncover and disrupt the plots of those willing to take up arms against others for the sake of jihad [holy war]?

Mordechai Kedar and David Yerushalmi, "Shari'a and Violence in American Mosques," *Middle East Quarterly*, Summer 2011, pp. 59–72. Copyright © 2011 by the Middle East Quarterly. All rights reserved. Reproduced by permission.

Root Causes and Enabling Mechanisms

While scholarly inquiry into the root causes and factors supportive of terrorism has accelerated since the September 11, 2001 attacks on the United States, there are few empirical studies that attempt to measure the relationship between specific variables and support for terrorism. To date, almost all of the professional and academic work in this field has been anecdotal surveys or case studies tracing backward through the personal profiles of terrorists and the socioeconomic and political environments from which they came.

One study by Quintan Wiktorowicz, assistant professor of international studies at Rhodes College and now on the staff of the National Security Council, noted that modern jihadists legitimize their violent activities by relying on the same textual works as their nonviolent Salafist [followers of the Sunni Islamic movement who exhibit high levels of Shari'a adherence] counterparts. However, the approach taken to these texts by the violent jihadist may be distinguished from that of the nonviolent Salafist insofar as the jihadist uses the principles advanced by both classical and modern Islamic scholars and ideologues and adapts them to modern situations in a way that provides a broader sanction for the permissible use of violence.

Further, in 2007, Paul Gill concluded that terrorist organizations seek societal support by creating a "culture of martyrdom" and that one theme common to suicide bombers was the support they received from a community that esteemed the concept of martyrdom. Thus, a complex dynamic is at work between a terrorist organization, society, and individuals with the interplay between these three dimensions enabling radicalization and terrorist attacks.

Another item that may help to understand the growth of modern jihadism appears in Marc Sageman's 2004 study, which found that 97 percent of jihadists studied had become increasingly devoted to forms of Salafist Islam highly adherent to Shari'a (Islamic law) while on their path to radicalization, despite many coming from less rigorous devotional levels during their youths. This increase in devotion to Salafist Islam was measured by outwardly observable behaviors such as wearing traditional Arabic, Pakistani, or Afghan clothing or growing a beard.

When viewed together, a picture emerges that may give researchers, as well as law enforcement officials, a way to monitor or potentially to predict where violent jihad may take root. Potential recruits who are swept up in this movement may find their inspiration and encouragement in a place with ready access to classic and modern literature that is positive toward jihad and violence, where highly Shari'a-adherent behavior is practiced, and where a society exists that in some form promotes a culture of martyrdom or at least engages in activities that are supportive of violent jihad. The mosque can be such a place.

The authors ... [tried] to determine ... [if] a correlation exists between ... Shari'a adherence in American mosques and the presence of violence-positive materials at those mosques.

That the mosque is a societal apparatus that might serve as a support mechanism for violent jihad may seem self-evident, but for it to be a useful means for measuring radicalization requires empirical evidence. A 2007 study by the New York city police department noted that, in the context of the mosque, high levels of Shari'a adherence, termed "Salafi ideology" by the authors of the report, may relate to support for violent jihad. Specifically, it found that highly Shari'a-adherent mosques have played a prominent role in radicalization. Another study found a relationship between frequency of mosque attendance and a predilection for supporting suicide attacks but discovered no empirical evidence linking support for suicide bombings to some measure of religious devotion (defined and measured by frequency of prayer).

However, the study suffers from a major methodological flaw, namely, reliance on self-reporting of prayer frequency. Muslims would be under social and psychological pressure to report greater prayer frequency because their status as good or pious believers is linked to whether they fulfill the religious obligation to pray five times a day. This piety is not dependent on regular mosque attendance as Muslims are permitted to pray outside of a mosque environment whenever necessary. Hence, the pressure to over-report exists for self-reporting of prayer frequency but is not present in self-reporting of frequency of mosque attendance, which is a measure of both coalitional or group commitment and religious devotion.

Thus, there is a need for the study and corroboration of a relationship between high levels of Shari'a adherence as a form of religious devotion and coalitional commitment, Islamic literature that shows violence in a positive light, and institutional support for violent jihad. By way of filling this lacuna [gap], the authors of this article undertook a survey specifically designed to determine empirically whether a correlation exists between observable measures of religious devotion linked to Shari'a adherence in American mosques and the presence of violence-positive materials at those mosques. The survey also sought to ascertain whether a correlation exists between the presence of violence-positive materials at a mosque and the promotion of jihadism by the mosque's leadership through recommending the study of these materials or other manifest behaviors.

Identifying Shari'a-Adherent Behaviors

Shari'a is the Islamic system of law based primarily on two sources held by Muslims to be respectively direct revelation from God and divinely inspired: the Qur'an and the Sunna (sayings, actions, and traditions of Muhammad). There are other jurisprudential sources for Shari'a derived from the legal rulings of Islamic scholars. These scholars, in turn, may be adherents of differing schools of Islamic jurisprudence. Notwithstanding those differences, the divergence at the level of actual law is, given the fullness of the *corpus juris* [body of law], confined to relatively few marginal issues. Thus, there is general unity and agreement across the Sunni-Shiite divide and across the various Sunni *madh'habs* (jurisprudential schools) on core normative behaviors.

Surveyors were asked to observe and record selected behaviors deemed to be Shari'a-adherent. These behaviors were selected precisely because they constitute observable and measurable practices of an orthodox form of Islam as opposed to internalized, non-observable articles of faith. Such visible modes of conduct are considered by traditionalists to have been either exhibited or commanded by Muhammad as recorded in the Sunna and later discussed and preserved in canonical Shari'a literature. The selected behaviors are among the most broadly accepted by legal practitioners of Islam and are not those practiced only by a rigid subgroup within Islam—Salafists, for example.

Among the behaviors observed at the mosques and scored as Shari'a-adherent were: (a) women wearing the *hijab* (head covering) or *niqab* (full-length shift covering the entire female form except for the eyes); (b) gender segregation during mosque prayers; and (c) enforcement of straight prayer lines. Behaviors that were not scored as Shari'a-adherent included: (a) women wearing just a modern *hijab*, a scarf-like covering that does not cover all of the hair, or no covering; (b) men and women praying together in the same room; and (c) no enforcement by the imam, lay leader, or worshipers of straight prayer lines.

The normative importance of a woman's hair covering is evidenced by two central texts, discussed at length below, *Reli-*

ance of the Traveller and *Fiqh as-Sunna* (Law of the Sunna), both of which express agreement on the obligation of a woman to wear the *hijab*:

> There is no such dispute over what constitutes a woman's *aurah* [private parts/nakedness]. It is stated that her entire body is *aurah* and must be covered, except her hands and face ... God does not accept the prayer of an adult woman unless she is wearing a head covering (*khimar, hijab*).
>
> The nakedness of a woman (even if a young girl) consists of the whole body except the face and hands. The nakedness of a woman is that which invalidates the prayer if exposed. . . . It is recommended for a woman to wear a covering over her head (*khimar*), a full length shift, and a heavy slip under it that does not cling to the body.

The severe material, by contrast, largely consists of relatively recent texts written by ideologues, rather than Shari'a scholars.

In a similar fashion, Shari'a requires that the genders be separated during prayers. While both *Reliance of the Traveller* and *Fiqh as-Sunna* express a preference that women should pray at home rather than the mosque, they agree that if women do pray in the mosque, they should pray in lines separate from the men. Additionally, authoritative Shari'a literature agrees that the men's prayer lines should be straight, that men should be close together within those lines, and that the imam should enforce prayer line alignment.

Sanctioned Violence

The mosques surveyed contained a variety of texts, ranging from contemporary printed pamphlets and handouts to classic texts of the Islamic canon. From the perspective of promoting violent jihad, the literature types were ranked in the survey from severe to moderate to nonexistent. The texts selected were all written to serve as normative and instructive tracts and are not scriptural. This is important because a believer is free to understand scripture literally, figuratively, or merely poetically when it does not have a normative or legal gloss provided by Islamic jurisprudence.

The moderate-rated literature was authored by respected Shari'a religious and/or legal authorities; while expressing positive attitudes toward violence, it was predominantly concerned with the more mundane aspects of religious worship and ritual. The severe material, by contrast, largely consists of relatively recent texts written by ideologues, rather than Shari'a scholars, such as Abul Ala Maududi and Sayyid Qutb. These, as well as materials published and disseminated by the Islamist Muslim Brotherhood, are primarily, if not exclusively, aimed at using Islam to advance a violent political agenda.

Maududi (1903–79), for one, believed that it was legitimate to wage violent jihad against "infidel colonizers" in order to gain independence and spread Islam. His *Jihad in Islam*, found in many of the mosques surveyed, instructed followers to employ force in pursuit of a Shari'a-based order:

> These [Muslim] men who propagate religion are not mere preachers or missionaries, but the functionaries of God [so that they may be witnesses for the people], and it is their duty to wipe out oppression, mischief, strife, immorality, high handedness, and unlawful exploitation from the world by force of arms.

Similarly, Qutb's *Milestones* serves as the political and ideological backbone of the current global jihad movement. Qutb, for example, sanctions violence against those who stand in the way of Islam's expansion:

> If someone does this [prevents others from accepting Islam], then it is the duty of Islam to fight him until either he is killed or until he declares his submission.

These materials differ from other severe- and moderate-rated materials because they are not Islamic legal texts per se but rather are polemical works seeking to advance a politicized Islam through violence, if necessary. Nor are these authors recognized Shari'a scholars.

The same cannot be said for some classical works that are also supportive of violence in the name of Islam. Works by several respected jurists and scholars from the four major Sunni schools of jurisprudence, dating from the eighth to fourteenth centuries, are all in agreement that violent jihad against non-Muslims is a religious obligation. Such behavior is normative, legally-sanctioned violence not confined to modern writers with a political axe to grind. Nor does its presence in classical Muslim works make it a relic of some medieval past. While *Umdat as-Salik* (*Reliance of the Traveller*) may have been compiled in the fourteenth century, al-Azhar University, perhaps the preeminent center of Sunni learning in the world, stated in its 1991 certification of the English translation that the book "conforms to the practice and faith of the orthodox Sunni community." While addressing a host of theological matters and detailed instructions as to how Muslims should order their daily routine to demonstrate piety and commitment to Islam, this certified, authoritative text spends eleven pages expounding on the applicability of jihad as violence directed against non-Muslims, stating for example:

> The caliph . . . makes war upon Jews, Christians, and Zoroastrians . . . provided he has first invited them to enter Islam in faith and practice, and if they will not, then invited them to enter the social order of Islam by paying the non-Muslim poll tax.

> The caliph fights all other peoples until they become Muslim . . . because they are not a people with a book, nor honored as such, and are not permitted to settle with paying the poll tax.

The *Fiqh as-Sunna* and *Tafsir Ibn Kathir* are examples of works that were rated "moderate" for purposes of this survey. The former, which focuses primarily on the internal Muslim community, the family, and the individual believer and not on violent jihad, was especially moderate in its endorsement of violence. Relatively speaking, the *Fiqh as-Sunna* expresses a more restrained view of violent jihad, in that it does not explicitly call for a holy war against the West even though it understands the Western influence on Islamic governments as a force that is destructive to Islam itself.

The survey's findings . . . were that 51 percent of mosques had texts that . . . advocated the use of violence.

Nonetheless, such texts do express positive views toward the use of violence against "the other," as expressed in the following:

> Ibn Abbas reported that the Prophet, upon whom be peace, said, "The ties of Islam and the principles of the religion are three, and whoever leaves one of them becomes an unbeliever, and his blood becomes lawful: testifying that there is no god except God, the obligatory prayers, and the fast of Ramadan.". . . Another narration states, "If anyone leaves one of [the three principles], by God he becomes an unbeliever, and no voluntary deeds or recompense will be accepted from him, and his blood and wealth become lawful." This is a clear indication that such a person is to be killed.

Similarly in *Tafsir Ibn Kathir*:

> Perform jihad against the disbelievers with the sword, and be harsh with the hypocrites with words, and this is the jihad performed against them.

The survey's findings . . . were that 51 percent of mosques had texts that either advocated the use of violence in the pursuit of a Shari'a-based political order or advocated violent jihad as a duty that should be of paramount importance to a Muslim; 30 percent had only texts that were moderately supportive of violence like the *Tafsir Ibn Kathir* and *Fiqh as-Sunna*; 19 percent had no violent texts at all. . . .

Broader Policy Implications

The conclusions to be drawn from this survey are dismal at best, offering empirical support for previous anecdotal studies on the connection between highly Shari'a-adherent mosques and political violence in the name of Islam. The mosques where there were greater indicators of Shari'a adherence were more likely to contain materials that conveyed a positive attitude toward employing violent jihad against the West and non-Muslims. The fact that spiritual sanctioners who help individuals become progressively more radicalized are connected to highly Shari'a-adherent mosques is another cause for deep concern. In almost every instance, the imams at the mosques where violence-positive materials were available recommended that worshipers study texts that promoted violence.

The survey also demonstrates that there are mosques and mosque-going Muslims who are interested in a non-Shari'a-centric Islam where tolerance of the other, at least as evidenced by the absence of jihad-promoting literature, is the norm. Mosques where violence-positive literature was not present exhibited significantly fewer indicators of orthodox, Shari'a-adherent behaviors and were also significantly less likely to promote violent jihad or invite speakers supportive of violent jihad. These non-Shari'a-centric mosques may provide a foundation from which a reformed Islam and its followers can more completely integrate into liberal, Western citizenship.

The results of this survey do not indicate the percentage of American Muslims that actually attend mosques with any regularity, nor does it reveal what relative percentage of American Muslims demonstrate Shari'a-adherent or non-adherent behaviors. Moreover, although this study shows that imams at Shari'a-adherent mosques recommend studying violence-positive materials and utilize their mosques for support of violent jihad, it does not capture the individual attendees' attitudes toward religiously sanctioned violence. However, it is at least reasonable to conclude that worshipers at such mosques are more sympathetic to the message of the literature present at those mosques and to what is being preached there. A follow-up survey of individual mosque attendees would provide insight regarding the relationship, if any, between Shari'a-adherence on the individual level and the individual's attitude toward violent jihad. . . .

Unfortunately, the results of the current survey strongly suggest that Islam—as it is generally practiced in mosques across the United States—continues to manifest a resistance to the kind of tolerant religious and legal framework that would allow its followers to make a sincere affirmation of liberal citizenship. This survey provides empirical support for the view that mosques across America, as institutional and social settings for mosque-going Muslims, are at least resistant to social cooperation with non-Muslims. Indeed, the overwhelming majority of mosques surveyed promoted literature supportive of violent jihad and a significant number invited speakers known to have promoted violent jihad and other behaviors that are inconsistent with a reasonable construct of liberal citizenship.

This survey suggests that, first and foremost, Muslim community leaders must take a more active role in educating their own faith community about the dangers associated with providing a safe haven for violent literature and its promotion—whether that safe haven is the mosque or the social club. These results also suggest that researchers and counterterrorist specialists should pay closer attention to the use and exploitation of classic Islamic legal doctrine and jurisprudence for recruiting and generating a commitment to violence against the perceived enemies of Islam. Finally, these findings should engender at least an interest among researchers to begin to study carefully Muslim attitudes toward citizenship and violence but one that differentiates between those who are Shari'a-adherent and those who are not. And, among Shari'a adherents, this future survey data must be sensitive to the distinction between traditionalism, orthodoxy, and Salafism, along with the more obvious sect distinctions, such as between Sunnis and Shiites.

Sharia Law in the United States Leads Americans One Step Closer to Islamist Conquest

JanSuzanne Krasner

JanSuzanne Krasner is a writer for American Thinker.

The incompatibility of Islamic sharia law with secular courts stems from the underpinning of Islamism—the unyielding union of the laws and punishments of the Qu'ran and Hadiths with the country's legal and political system. Sharia law is the legislation of these religious and criminal rules, which *rejects* America's constitutional secularism and legal penalties.

The Qu'ran commands Muslims to change secular laws to conform to sharia, eventually establishing Islamic law worldwide. Islamic courts want their fatwas [legal decree by Islamic scholar] to supersede the civil and criminal laws, untying Muslims from civil secular courts.

The facts reveal that in 2008, when the first sharia court was recognized in the U.K. [United Kingdom], within one year, over 85 recognized sharia courts were established within the U.K.'s Tribunal Court system. The problem with this rapidly spreading dogma is that several of these courts have issued some fatwas that are completely incompatible with British and European law.

As Islam is a male-dominated ideology, the laws of the Qu'ran make half of its devotees, its female population, second-class citizens. This inequality has drawn recent [2011] attention to the need for additional British legislation to rein in these courts so they abide by British law.

It appears that once any legal system opens its doors to Islamic law, that door will be hard to close . . . and eventually, the only thing missing will be a parallel Islamic government.

The possibility that Muslim-only towns and urban enclaves could be created in the U.S. seems unimaginable to most Americans.

But even with this reality in front of Americans, there are still many who insist that our laws will prevent such circumstances from ever occurring in the U.S. And because of this nonchalant attitude, there are numbers of people, both Muslim and non-Muslim, who believe that sharia law is not a threat to non-Muslim Americans or to the Western liberal democratic rule of law.

Sharia Law Is in the United States

The possibility that Muslim-only towns and urban enclaves could be created in the U.S. seems unimaginable to most Americans, but it already is a reality. Just travel 150 miles northwest of New York City to the woods of the western Catskills, and you will find Islamberg, a private Muslim community founded in 1980 by Sheikh Syed Mubarik Ali Shah Gilani. Sheikh Gilani is said to be one of the founders of Jamaat al-Fuqra, a terrorist organization believed to be responsible for dozens of bombings and murders in the U.S. and abroad.

Islamberg is only one of twenty to thirty Muslim-only communities and training compounds that this Pakistani group supports through Muslim affiliates in America. This radical group has purchased land in isolated areas close to city networks and infrastructure. Jamaat al-Fuqra now has sites in Alabama, Georgia, Oklahoma, South Carolina, Tennessee, Virginia, Pennsylvania, California, Washington, Colorado, Michigan, and Illinois, as well as Canada, Venezuela, and Trinidad.

The sharia debate in the U.S. is heating up as more and more Americans are reacting to lawyers requesting rulings based on sharia law, and local judges agreeing to make them. This has happened in a New Jersey divorce case, a Maryland child custody case, and most recently in a Florida property case. These cases are now a precedent for other American-Muslim communities. In addition, according to the Center for Security Policy study that was published in May 2011, there are actually over fifty Appellate Court cases from 23 states that all involve conflicts between sharia law and American state law.

There are numbers of Muslim community leaders challenging the delicate line between religious freedom and the laws against state religion by petitioning in favor of living under sharia law. The moment one court allows the establishment of an independently ruled enclave, other courts in liberal cities across the nation will petition for the same opportunity.

Another example of efforts to usurp the Constitution are the actions of the global Organization of Islamic Cooperation (OIC), whose main agenda is to have "hate speech" laws enforced against anyone who criticizes Islam. And, unfortunately, there are those determined to enforce sharia on their own who attack and murder any nearby dissenters. The Qu'ran justifies and protects these people's violence by declaring that it is blasphemous to mock or degrade any component of Islam. According to sharia law, such activity is punishable by death.

It is this ongoing effort to shut down public criticism of Islam that presents the gravest danger to America—one that the Muslim Brotherhood and its Salafist organizations regard as key to limiting individual rights over the rights of the community. The Council on American-Islamic Relations (CAIR), along with other Islamic activist groups, continues to push back, often with demonization of character and follow-up lawsuits. Recently, intimidation and character assassination have been used against U.S. politicians who question Islamism or want hearings on issues relating to radical Islamic terrorism, along with those Congressmen who introduce state legislation to ban all foreign law.

Preventing Sharia Through Legislation

The Court of Appeals is the system used to review lower court decisions and believed by some to be the stopgap against foreign law, including sharia, from entering our legal system. However, some Islamic cases that have reached the Appellate Court for review have retained the sharia rulings even in the face of sharia's contradiction to American civil law.

The U.S. is heading towards dangerous territory if its citizens buy into the twisting of constitutional amendments. Indeed, what everyone really needs is the interpretations of the laws as they are written in order to prevent the encroachment of Islamism into the court system.

The establishment of sharia courts within the arbitration laws is a leading objective of every peace-loving, kindhearted, moderate male Muslim. I have asked several male American Muslims whom I know, some living very happily in my community and in the U.S., what their one greatest wish is. The answer is always the same: "Everyone should be a Muslim."

The line must be drawn in states' legislatures, not in the courts. It is imperative that we recognize the differences between the religion of Islam and the ideology of Islamism. Political correctness is leading to interpretations of the Constitution and its amendments that are pushing America across that line.

If non-Muslim Americans do not recognize how close they are to the precipice, then they are beyond a shadow of a doubt going to fall victims to an Islamic conquest. Time is running out.

Sharia Law Is a Danger to Civil Society

Cully Stimson

Cully Stimson, a former deputy assistant defense secretary, is a senior legal fellow at the Heritage Foundation.

Does Sharia law allow a husband to rape his wife, even in America? A New Jersey trial judge thought so. In a recently overturned case, a "trial judge found as a fact that defendant committed conduct that constituted a sexual assault" but did not hold the defendant liable because the defendant believed he was exercising his rights over the victim. Fortunately, a New Jersey appellate court reversed the trial judge. But make no mistake about it: this is no isolated incident. We will see more cases here in the United States where others attempt to impose Sharia law, under the guise of First Amendment protections, as a defense against crimes and other civil violations.

Sharia Law Permits Wife Abuse

In *S.D. v. M.J.R.*, the plaintiff, a Moroccan Muslim woman, lived with her Moroccan Muslim husband in New Jersey. She was repeatedly beaten and raped by her husband over the course of several weeks. While the plaintiff was being treated for her injuries at a hospital, a police detective interviewed her and took photographs of her injuries. Those photographs depicted injuries to plaintiff's breasts, thighs and arm, bruised lips, eyes and right check. Further investigation established there were blood stains on the pillow and sheets of plaintiff's bed.

The wife sought a permanent restraining order, and a New Jersey trial judge held a hearing in order to decide whether to issue the order. Evidence at trial established, among other things, that the husband told his wife. "You must do whatever I tell you to do. I want to hurt your flesh" and "this is according to our religion. You are my wife, I c[an] do anything to you." The police detective testified about her findings, and some of the photographs were entered into evidence.

The ruling ... goes to the heart of the controversy about the insidious spread of Sharia law.

The defendant's Imam testified that a wife must comply with her husband's sexual demands and he refused to answer whether, under Islamic law, a husband must stop his sexual advances on his wife if she says "no."

The trial judge found that most of the criminal acts were indeed proved, but nonetheless denied the permanent retraining order. This judge held that the defendant could not be held responsible for the violent sexual assaults of his wife because he did not have the specific intent to sexually assault his wife, and because his actions were "consistent with his [religious] practices." In other words, the judge refused to issue the permanent restraining order because under Sharia law, this Muslim husband had a "right" to rape his wife

Besides the fact that the ruling is wrong as a legal matter, and offensive beyond words, it goes to the heart of the controversy about the insidious spread of Sharia law—the goal of radical Islamic extremists. Fortunately, the New Jersey appellate court refused to tolerate the trial judge's "mistaken" and unsustainable decision. The appellate court chastised the trial judge's ruling, holding among other things that he held an "unnecessarily dismissive view of defendant's acts of domestic violence," and that his views of the facts in the case "may have been colored by his perception that ... they were culturally acceptable and thus not actionable—a view we soundly reject." Although appellate courts typically defer to findings of fact by trial judges, under the circumstances, this appellate court correctly refused to do so, and reversed the trial court and ordered the permanent restraining order to issue.

So-called "cultural defenses" have existed in other contexts for a long while and, for the most part, such defenses have been rejected.

The truth is that imposition of Sharia law in the United States, especially when mixed with a perverted sense of political correctness, poses a danger to civil society. Just last year, a Muslim man in Buffalo, New York beheaded his wife in what appeared to be an honor killing, again using his faith to justify his actions. It is doubtful that the domestic violence and rape in this recently overturned case will be the last Americans see of Sharia being impermissibly used to justify brutal acts on our soil. As former Assistant Secretary of Defense Frank Gaffney wrote recently:

> Sharia is no less toxic when it comes to the sorts of democratic government and civil liberties guaranteed by the U.S. Constitution. According to this legal code of Saudi Arabia and Iran, only Allah can make laws, and only a theocrat can properly administer them, ultimately on a global basis.

Cultural Defenses Should Be Rejected

The trial opinion in this case shows that, indeed, the global reach of Sharia law is expanding. The trial court allowed the testimony of an Imam to be entered so that his account of Sharia's standards could supersede the standards set by the New Jersey legislature. This is not just about cultural defenses, which by themselves are not proper under United States law, but about giving up control of the law to a religious code citizens of this country have no control over, a theocratic code world famous for its antidemocratic, sexist nature and its human rights abuses.

So-called "cultural defenses" have existed in other contexts for a long while and, for the most part, such defenses have been rejected. As a domestic violence prosecutor in San Diego, I ran across a case where the accused was charged with assault for punching his girlfriend, and the defense wanted to introduce an expert in Latin cultures. The expert was to testify that in Latin culture, it is acceptable for a man to strike "his woman" as punishment as long as it doesn't cause serious lasting injury. This was rejected outright by the court, as it should have been. These attempts are not uncommon, but the cultural relativism they espouse is different than the more dangerous trend here.

In *S.D. v. M.J.R.*, the husband's defense for sexually assaulting his wife was not just another attempt to erode the protection of our own social mores. The specific threat that comes from attempting to establish Sharia law in the United States is that justification for doing so has been couched in the protections of the First Amendment. As noted by the appeals court in its decision overturning what amounted to the replacement of New Jersey's rape law with Sharia, "the judge determined to except [the] defendant from the operation of the State's statutes as the result of his religious beliefs." Doing so was contrary to several Supreme Court decisions, which hold that an individual's responsibility to obey generally applicable law—particularly those that regulate socially harmful conduct—cannot be made contingent up on his or her religious beliefs.

The U.S. Constitution cannot and should not be used to subvert legislatures and allow brutes such as the husband in this case to harm others simply because their actions are legal under Sharia law. It was impermissible for the trial court to act as it did in this case, and the appellate judges very correctly overturned the ruling below. This is not the last we will hear of such attempts, however, as Sharia-loving extremists are determined to establish an Islamic Caliphate around the world, especially in America. As Andy McCarthy has written, "Our enemies are those who want Sharia to supplant American law and Western culture." We cannot allow that to happen.

Demonizing Sharia Law Is Counterproductive

Reuel Marc Gerecht

Reuel Marc Gerecht is a senior fellow at the Foundation for Defense of Democracies and a contributing editor at the Weekly Standard.

After recent [2010] conversations with *The Atlantic's* Jeffrey Goldberg and others who are of a more conservative bent, I started to reflect on Western scholarship and American conservative commentary on Islam. Western historiography of Islam provides a treasure-trove of sympathetic and hostile criticism of the Middle East's last-horn, earth-shaking faith. A huge body of modern Western scholarship has sought, more often from curious sympathy than malice, to answer the quintessentially liberal question about Islam: "What went wrong?"

Sharia Law Is Not Behind the Terrorist Threat

And things going astray is a good way to look at some prominent conservative commentary. Although liberals have been quick and careless in hurling accusations of Islamophobia at opponents of the Ground Zero/Park 51 cultural center, there is something historically and philosophically amiss in some conservative ruminations about the Islamic faith. It really shouldn't be so hard to oppose Islamic militancy, push back forcefully against those who downplay the threat of Al Qaeda as well as a nuclear Iran, and, at the same time, not suggest that all Muslims are, basically, nuts.

There is, to be sure, absolutely nothing wrong with non-Muslim Americans engaging in a debate about faith and violence that ranges far and wide. Western history offers a lengthy chronicle that encourages an exploration of why devout men kill for God; Christian-Muslim parallels provide a lens through which to see where—and where not—sincere believers in the Almighty have interpreted how violence and religion intermarry. So, no, there is no sin in non-Muslims querying Muslims about why so many terrorists tend to be Muslim and why those terrorists advertise their acts of violence as a defense of their faith. There is nothing wrong with asking why so many Muslims have such a difficult time saying that Palestinian suicide bombers have committed acts of evil. There is nothing wrong, either, in asking why it is that Islamic radicals melted two skyscrapers and blew out a side of the Pentagon and yet prompted so little soulful reflection, produced no Émile Zola, no Captain Dreyfus [Emile Zola wrote a defense of the falsely accused Jewish French army officer, Alfred Dreyfus, who was convicted by anti-Semites]. Short of that, Muslims in the West at least ought to have a few [*New York Times* columnists] Thomas Friedmans and Roger Cohens crankily telling them what a mess they've made.

But all of these serious Islamic problems aside (and any Westerner aware of the quantity of blood that Westerners themselves spilled making the world modern really ought to exercise a bit of charity when it comes to Islam's travails), we still ought to be concerned when prominent American conservatives—and here I'm thinking first and foremost of Newt Gingrich—blur the line between militant Muslims and the everyday faithful. When Gingrich, whom I've long admired and had the pleasure of working with, gave a much-noted speech at the American Enterprise Institute in which he stated. "I believe Sharia is a mortal threat to the survival of freedom in the United States and in the world as we know it. . . . I think it's that straightforward and that real," I could only say in response, "String Theory is dangerous": Gingrich was looking for an explanation for the Islamic terrorist threat, but, like many on the right, looking in the wrong places. Neatly tying it all together, Gingrich and others have alighted upon the Muslim Holy Law, the Sharia, as the source of all that bedevils the Middle East, and us.

This is hardly the place for a disquisition on Sharia, or how it's evolved over the centuries. Suffice to say, even some Muslim theologians have seen the strain of despotism in Islamic history as being connected to the static and authoritarian nature of Islamic legal practice. Still, I've spent a lot of time sitting with Shiite and Sunni clerics who were teaching Sharia and opining about daily life, and such schooling didn't strike me then, and still doesn't, as a good laboratory for terrorists, which is why, I suspect, so few terrorists have had any proper clerical training. A rigorous Islamic education may make you a killjoy, but it doesn't make you a terrorist. If the empirical record tells us anything, it's that a skimpy Islamic education combined with a mediocre—even a decent—Western education seems much more likely to produce an explosive mix.

Westerners, especially Europeans, are quite right to be outraged by the importation of Sharia practices to their shores.

Muslim Clergy Can Be a Voice of Reason

When Westerners, however well-intentioned, start suggesting that Muslim law supplies the foundation for Islamic terrorism, it immediately conveys to Muslims, even secularized Muslims, that Westerners think all Muslims are disordered, that the only route to salvation runs through a renunciation of their faith (that is, they ought to become the mirror-image of Westerners who go to church every so often). Whatever vestigial pride Muslims may have in their religious law (most Muslims aren't particularly fastidious or knowledgeable about the Sharia, but nevertheless have an understandable historic affection for it), gets crudely pummeled by such commentators.

The blanket demonization of the Holy Law can lead one to view Iraq's Grand Ayatollah Ali Sistani, the most revered Shiite thinker in the world, and one who tried desperately and selflessly to keep his country from descending into internecine savagery, as a bigot and a terrorist engine. The same would be true for the late Grand Ayatollah Ali Montazeri, the spiritual father of Iran's Green Movement and the nemesis of Ali Khamenei, Iran's ruler, himself a very mediocre student of the Sharia.

True, the Holy Law applied can be ugly, not least for women. Westerners, especially Europeans, are quite right to be outraged by the importation of Sharia practices to their shores. And Westerners should cast a very dim eye on any financial institution that sets up Sharia-compliant offices that could, if left unchecked, discreetly normalize anti-Semitic practices in big global institutions. Westerners can only hope that progressive Muslim jurists, who briefly sprouted in the nineteenth century, once more gain force among the faithful. But we should not make the great philosophical and historical mistake of seeing even the staunchly conservative clerical elite of the Muslim world as the handmaidens of Islamic terrorism. If, indeed, Islamic terrorism comes to an end, it will probably be because these men have united to say finally and clearly that a devout Muslim's distaste for Western values and "cultural imperialism" does not, after all, justify murder.

The intellectual peregrinations of Saudi Wahhabism, the mother-ship of Sunni Islamic terrorism, may be frightful, but, even in Saudi Arabia, the best bet for ending this plague may likely be found among the ranks of its reactionary clergy. What Westerners should dream of is not the elimination of the influence of the Sharia in Muslim lands, but the triumph of a more competitive mindset among those who adhere to the Law. If Saudi Arabia, at home and abroad, would just welcome Hanafis, the most open-minded of Sunni Islam's law schools, it would be an enormous triumph over Wahhabi intolerance and the hatred that spews forth from that oil-rich land.

The traumatic Westernization of Islam continues.

Free-lancing, perfectly modern rebels like Osama bin Laden, who believe they alone have the right to interpret God's message, will no doubt storm forth now and then, but they would have a much harder time if the Sunni clergy were arrayed openly and loudly against them. When, for instance, Iran and Lebanon's Shiites fell in love with holy war and martyrdom, prominent Shiite clerics went the other way. Among the Shiite faithful, suicide bombing had a short run. Hezbollah's Hassan Nasrallah is a wicked zealot who loves to kill Jews, but he is, like his counterparts in Iran, Ali Khamenei and Mahmoud Ahmadinejad, of no religious standing. As counterintuitive as it seems to some Americans, it may be divines who are among the most effective opponents of such men.

Muslims Are Being Westernized

Misunderstanding Islam's internal problems and miscasting the Sharia and its clerical custodians as our primary enemies aren't, however, the biggest problems with some American conservative commentary. Many conservatives—and liberals— utterly fail to appreciate the extraordinary continuing power of Western, especially American, culture among Muslims. Declinism may be all the rage among trend-chasers in the West, but the apocalyptic tactics of Osama bin Laden and his followers offer, among other things, evidence that we, the West, have been winning the war for the hearts of everyday Muslims. Among Muslims fixed to their computers and televisions, we still embody both hope and hell on earth. As Khomeini put it so well, we remain the satanic whisperer, who seduces men—and especially women—from the righteous path.

Contrary to what one regularly reads on conservative websites, we are not yet losing this war. Iran's pursuit of a nuclear weapon and the determined proselytizing of the Muslim Brotherhood in the Middle East and among Muslim immigrants in the West are efforts to turn back the tide. But modernity is relentless. The traumatic Westernization of Islam continues. That Westernization led to the Islamic revolution in Iran and to Osama bin Laden, but it also leads, even more powerfully, to a world where Muslims—specially Muslim women—aspire to a more prosperous and democratic way of life. We have reasons to hope that Islam's passage will be less bloody than our own, though we should prepare, as Gingrich constantly and wisely warns us, for its being worse.

But we shouldn't see enemies where they are not. The Holy Law is, as it's always been, what Muslims make of it. In the titanic struggle within Islam between those who fear modernity and those who embrace it, we would do well not to make the clergy our foes. They will go, as they always have done, where the majority of Muslims take them. Like Ayatollah Khomeini before him, bin Laden once thought that most Muslims would rise up to defend his cause. Both gentlemen were wrong. Westerners and most Muslims may not (yet) share with the same intensity and priority that many values, but we share enough to provide considerable hope that the "clash of civilizations" will end, as Grand Ayatollah Sistani no doubt wants it to, in a suspicious, at times tense, but peaceful and prosperous co-existence.

Attempts to Ban Sharia Law Are Based on Ignorance and Islamophobia

Abed Awad, interviewed by Justin Elliott

Abed Awad is a New Jersey–based attorney and member of the adjunct faculties at Rutgers Law School and Pace Law School. Justin Elliott is a reporter for Salon.

Last week [February 2011] in Tennessee, a Republican legislator introduced a bill that would make following sharia—Islamic law—a felony, punishable by up to 15 years in prison. How such a law would be enforced is not clear; furthermore, it's probably unconstitutional.

It is clear, though, that an anti-sharia movement is growing in the United States. Last year Oklahoma voters approved a measure that bars courts from considering sharia. Similar measures have now been introduced or passed in at least 13 other states. Indeed, anti-Muslim political operatives have been warning of "creeping sharia" and "Islamist lawfare" for years, though the anti-sharia efforts have gained new prominence in recent months.

Sharia Is Both Law and Methodology

But even basic facts about sharia—what is it? how is it used in American courts?—are hard to come by. So I decided to talk to Abed Awad, a New Jersey-based attorney and an expert on sharia who regularly handles cases that involve Islamic law. He is also a member of the adjunct faculties at Rutgers Law School and Pace Law School. He recently answered my questions via e-mail.

Abed Awad, interviewed by Justin Elliott, "What Sharia Law Actually Means," *Salon.com*, February 26, 2011. Copyright © 2011 by Salon.com. This article first appeared in Salon .com, at http://www.salon.com. An online version remains in the Salon archives. Reprinted with permission.

Justin Elliott: Can you define sharia—is it a specific body of laws?

Abed Awad: Sharia is more than simply "law" in the prescriptive sense. It is also a methodology through which a jurist engages the religious texts to ascertain divine will. As a jurist-made law, the outcome of this process of ascertaining divine will is called fiqh (positive law), which is the moral and legal anchor of a Muslim's total existence. Sharia governs every aspect of an observant Muslim's life. The sharia juristic inquiry begins with the Quran and the Sunna. The Quran is the Muslim Holy Scripture—like the New Testament for Christians or the Old Testament for the Jews. The Sunna is essentially the prophetic example embodied in the sayings and conduct of the Prophet Mohammed.

In the 19th century, Western colonialism decimated the sharia legal system, replacing it with Western codes.

After the two primary sources of Islamic law, the Quran and the Sunna, the two main secondary sources of Islamic law are: (1) ijma (consensus of the scholars and jurists, and sometimes the entire community), and (2) qiyas (reasoning by analogy to one of the higher sources). Other secondary sources of Islamic law are juristic preference, public interest and custom. Sharia is extremely flexible and subject to various interpretations. In the 19th century, Western colonialism decimated the sharia legal system, replacing it with Western codes. This caused a serious decline in the community of jurists. In addition, there is today a debate that revolves around the failure of the modern jurists—not the system of sharia—to develop the sharia to adapt with the current circumstances of modernity.

How often does sharia come up in U.S. courts? Has there been an uptick recently?

It comes up often because the American-Muslim community is growing. With an estimated 8 million Americans who adhere to Islam, it is only natural to see a rapid increase of Muslim litigants before American courts where sharia may be an issue—especially in family matters.

Can you give a couple examples of when sharia has come up in cases that you've handled?

In the past 12 years as an attorney, I have handled many cases with an Islamic law component. U.S. courts are required to regularly interpret and apply foreign law—including Islamic law—to everything from the recognition of foreign divorces and custody decrees to the validity of marriages, the enforcement of money judgments, probating an Islamic will and the damages element in a commercial dispute. Sharia is relevant in a U.S. court either as a foreign law or as a source of information to understand the expectations of the parties in a dispute.

Suppose a New York resident wife files for divorce in New York; her husband files for annulment in Egypt claiming the parties were never validly married. A New York judge must determine whether he has jurisdiction and whether state law governs this dispute. If the conflict of laws of New York requires that Egyptian law govern the issue of validity, the court would require expert testimony about Egyptian law that is based on Islamic law.

Another common use of sharia in American courts is in the enforcement of Muslim marriage contracts. Like the majority of Americans, Muslims opt for a religious marriage ceremony. In every Muslim marriage, the parties enter into a Muslim marriage contract. The contract includes a provision called mahr, which is a lump sum payment from the groom to the bride that, unless otherwise agreed, would be due at the time of the husband's death or the dissolution of the marriage. An American court would require expert testimony to understand what a mahr is, what a Muslim marriage contract is, and to better understand the expectations of the parties at the time of the contract. All of this would be necessary for the court to determine whether the contract is valid under state law.

She testified that her husband told her repeatedly that, according to his religion, she was obligated to submit to his sexual requests.

Foreign Law That Is Not Unconstitutional Can Be Considered in U.S. Courts

Is sharia used in U.S. courts any differently than other foreign or religious systems of law?

No, it is utilized the same way as Jewish law or canon law or any other law.

A lot of critics of sharia have cited a case in New Jersey in which a husband cited sharia to argue that he did not rape his wife. What happened in that case?

The case is *S.D. v. M.J.R.* It's not about sharia as much as it is about a state court judge who failed to follow New Jersey law. In this case, the plaintiff-wife sought a restraining order against her husband, alleging that his nonconsensual action constituted physical abuse. She testified that her husband told her repeatedly that, according to his religion, she was obligated to submit to his sexual requests.

The trial judge refused to issue the restraining order, finding that the defendant was operating under a religious belief that he was entitled to have marital relations with his wife whenever he wanted. Thus, he did not form the criminal intent to commit domestic violence. But, of course, the appellate court reversed the trial court decision, holding that the defendant's nonconsensual sexual intercourse with his wife was "unquestionably knowing, regardless of his view that his religion permitted him to act as he did." The appellate ruling is consistent with Islamic law, which prohibits spousal abuse, including nonconsensual sexual relations. A minority of Muslims mistakenly believe that a husband can discipline his wife with physical force in the interest of saving the marriage and avoiding divorce.

What about stoning, which critics also claim is part of sharia?

The Quran does not provide for the stoning of adulterers. The punishment prescribed in the Quran is lashing. However, there is a prophetic tradition that adopted the Jewish custom of stoning adulterers. Many people describe the American legal system as having a Judeo-Christian heritage. Does that mean that we will stone adulterers as required in the Bible? No.

As long as a provision in Jewish law, canon law or sharia does not offend our constitutional protections and public policy, courts will consider it. Otherwise, courts would not consider it. In other words, foreign law or religious law in American courts is considered within American constitutional strictures.

What do you make of these state-level efforts to ban consideration of sharia in American courts?

Other than the fact that such bans are unconstitutional—a federal court recently held that a ban would likely violate the Supremacy Clause and the First Amendment—they are a monumental waste of time. Our judges are equipped with the constitutional framework to refuse to recognize a foreign law. In the end, our Constitution is the law of the land.

The only explanation is that they appear to be driven by an agenda infused with hate, ignorance and Islamophobia intent on dehumanizing an entire religious community. That a dozen states are actively moving to adopt anti-sharia laws demonstrates that this is part of a pattern. This is not haphazard. Someone—a group of people—is trying to turn this into a national issue. I believe this will become an election issue. Are you with the sharia or with the U.S. Constitution? It is absurd.

The US Legal System Would Never Adopt Sharia Law

Wajahat Ali and Matthew Duss

Wajahat Ali is a researcher and writer at the Center for American Progress; Matthew Duss is national security editor at the Center for American Progress.

In the past year [as of March 2011], a group of conservative pundits and analysts have identified Sharia, or Islamic religious law, as a growing threat to the United States. These pundits and analysts argue that the steady adoption of Sharia's tenets is a strategy extremists are using to transform the United States into an Islamic state.

Conservatives Are Exaggerating the Sharia Threat

A number of state and national politicians have adopted this interpretation and 13 states are now considering the adoption of legislation forbidding Sharia. A bill in the Tennessee State Senate, for example, would make adherence to Sharia punishable by 15 years in jail. Former Speaker of the House of Representatives and potential presidential candidate Newt Gingrich has called for "a federal law that says Sharia law cannot be recognized by any court in the United States."

The fullest articulation of this "Sharia threat" argument, though, is in the September 2010 report "Sharia: The Threat to America," published by the conservative Center for Security Policy [CSP]. The authors claim that their report is "concerned with the preeminent totalitarian threat of our time: the legal-political-military doctrine known within Islam as

'Shariah.'" The report, according to its authors, is "designed to provide a comprehensive and articulate 'second opinion' on the official characterizations and assessments of this threat as put forth by the United States government."

The report, and the broader argument, is plagued by a significant contradiction. In the CSP report's introduction, the authors admit that Islamic moderates contest more conservative interpretations of Sharia:

> Sharia is the crucial fault line of Islam's internecine struggle. On one side of the divide are Muslim reformers and authentic moderates ... whose members embrace the Enlightenment's veneration of reason and, in particular, its separation of the spiritual and secular realms. On this side of the divide, Sharia is a reference point for a Muslim's personal conduct, not a corpus to be imposed on the life of a pluralistic society.

The authors later assert, however, that there is "ultimately but one shariah. It is totalitarian in character, incompatible with our Constitution and a threat to freedom here and around the world."

The initial concession that Muslims interpret Sharia in different ways is accurate and of course contradicts the later assertion that Sharia is totalitarian in nature.

According to the "Sharia threat" argument, all Muslims who practice any aspect of their faith are inherently suspect.

But by defining Sharia itself as the problem, and then asserting the authenticity of only the most extreme interpretations of Sharia, the authors are effectively arguing that the internecine struggle within Islam should be ceded to extremists. They also cast suspicion upon all observant Muslims.

It's important to understand that adopting such a flawed analysis would direct limited resources away from actual threats to the United States and bolster an anti-Muslim narrative that Islamist extremist groups find useful in recruiting.

It would also target and potentially alienate our best allies in the effort against radicalization: our fellow Americans who are Muslim. According to the "Sharia threat" argument, all Muslims who practice any aspect of their faith are inherently suspect since Sharia is primarily concerned with correct religious practice.

This brief will explain what Sharia really is and demonstrate how a misrepresentation and misunderstanding of Sharia—put forth in the CSP report and taken up by others—will both harm America's national security interests and threaten our constitutionally guaranteed freedoms.

What Is Sharia?

The CSP report defines Sharia as a "legal-political-military doctrine." But a Muslim would not recognize this definition— let alone a scholar of Islam and Muslim tradition. Muslim communities continue to internally debate how to practice Islam in the modern world even as they look to its general precepts as a guide to correct living and religious practice.

Most academics studying Islam and Muslim societies give a broad definition of Sharia. This reflects Muslim scholars struggling for centuries over how best to understand and practice their faith.

But these specialists do agree on the following:

- *Sharia is not static.* Its interpretations and applications have changed and continue to change over time.

- *There is no one thing called Sharia.* A variety of Muslim communities exist, and each understands Sharia in its own way. No official document, such as the Ten Commandments, encapsulates Sharia. It is the ideal law of

God as interpreted by Muslim scholars over centuries aimed toward justice, fairness, and mercy.

• *Sharia is overwhelmingly concerned with personal religious observance such as prayer and fasting, and not with national laws.*

Any observant Muslim would consider him or herself a Sharia adherent. It is impossible to find a Muslim who practices any ritual and does not believe himself or herself to be complying with Sharia. Defining Sharia as a threat, therefore, is the same thing as saying that all observant Muslims are a threat.

The CSP report authors—none of whom has any credentials in the study of Islam—concede this point in several places. In the introduction they say, "Shariah is a reference point for a Muslim's personal conduct, not a corpus to be imposed on the life of a pluralistic society." Yet the rest of the report contradicts this point.

The authors, in attempting to show that Sharia is a threat, construct a static, ahistorical, and unscholarly interpretation of Sharia that is divorced from traditional understandings and commentaries of the source texts.

The "Sharia threat" argument is based on an extreme type of scripturalism where one pulls out verses from a sacred text and argues that believers will behave according to that text. But this argument ignores how believers themselves understand and interpret that text over time.

The equivalent would be saying that Jews stone disobedient sons to death (Deut. 21:18–21) or that Christians slay all non-Christians (Luke 19:27). In a more secular context it is similar to arguing that the use of printed money in America is unconstitutional—ignoring the interpretative process of the Supreme Court.

In reality, Sharia is personal religious law and moral guidance for the vast majority of Muslims. Muslim scholars historically agree on certain core values of Sharia, which are theological and ethical and not political. Moreover, these core values are in harmony with the core values at the heart of America.

The fact that the Amman Message is a Sharia-based document shows the problem with the "Sharia threat" argument.

Muslims consider an interpretation of Sharia to be valid so long as it protects and advocates for life, property, family, faith, and intellect. Muslim tradition overwhelmingly accepts differences of opinion outside these core values, which is why Sharia has survived for centuries as an ongoing series of conversations. Sharia has served Muslims who have lived in every society and in every corner of the planet, including many Americans who have lived in our country from before our independence down to the present day.

Recent statements from Muslim religious authorities, such as the 2004 Amman Message, show the dynamic, interpretive tradition of Islam in practice. In fact, the Amman Message is a Sharia-based condemnation of violence. So if CSP wants Muslims to reject Sharia they are effectively arguing Muslims should reject nonviolence.

The fact that the Amman Message is a Sharia-based document shows the problem with the "Sharia threat" argument: By criminalizing Sharia they also criminalize the Sharia-based message of nonviolence in the Amman document.

It is surprising that a group claiming to be invested in American national security would suggest that we make nonviolent engagement criminal.

Suspicion Based on
Religious Misinterpretation

The CSP report's contradictions can only be resolved through unconstitutional means. And the authors propose doing so with no sense of irony.

They argue that believing Muslims should have their free speech and freedom of religion rights restricted: "In keeping with Article VI of the Constitution, extend bans currently in effect that bar members of hate groups such as the Ku Klux Klan from holding positions of trust in federal, state, or local governments or the armed forces of the United States to those who espouse or support Shariah."

The authors have already conceded that even mainstream Muslims espouse Sharia. So by the report's own analysis, CSP are recommending that even mainstream American Muslims, who follow Sharia in their personal lives, be prohibited from serving in the government or the armed forces.

The authors cite Koran verses that "are interpreted under Shariah to mean that anyone who does not accept Islam is unacceptable in the eyes of Allah and that he will send them to Hell," concluding, "When it is said that Shariah is a supremacist program, this is one of the bases for it."

It is no secret that many Christians interpret their own faith to mean that non-Christians are destined for Hell. Is this too a form of supremacism?

Many advocates of the "Sharia threat" also refer to taqiyya, an Arabic word that means concealing one's faith out of fear of death, to mean religiously justified lying. Not all Muslims subscribe to the theological concept of taqiyya, however. In fact, it is a minority opinion.

The charge of "taqqiya" is often deployed by "Sharia threat" advocates when confronted with evidence that refutes their thesis. Under this methodology one cannot trust any practicing Muslim. Even if a Muslim preaches and practices nonviolence the CSP authors would say that person is either not a true Muslim or is practicing taqiyya.

They have, in fact, used this tactic against Muslim-American leaders who advocate strong civic engagement. Responding to Imam Feisal Abdul Rauf's assertion that the proposed Park 51 Islamic Center in New York would be a venue for interfaith dialogue, CSP's Frank Gaffney wrote in *The Washington Times*: "To be sure, Imam Rauf is a skilled practitioner of the Shariah tradition of taqqiya, deception for the faith."

All Muslims are suspect simply by virtue of being Muslims.

While providing a mechanism for critics to ignore any disconfirming evidence, adopting such an interpretation of taqiyya would almost certainly result in every observant Muslim being branded a liar.

The authors of the CSP report are clearly aware of this, and they try to temper their conclusions: "This is not an argument for trusting or mistrusting someone in any particular instance," they write. "It is, though, an argument for professionals to be aware of these facts, to realize that they are dealing with an enemy whose doctrine allows—and at times even requires—them not to disclose fully all that they know and deliberately to misstate that which they know to be the truth."

In other words, all Muslims are suspect simply by virtue of being Muslims.

Biased Premises Lead to Bad Policy

The CSP report's premise is that Sharia is the problem and that observance of Sharia results in extremism. The authors do not acknowledge that Sharia is something the extremists are attempting to claim.

This purposeful misconstruction of the security issues America faces ignores multiple data points and turns all Muslims into traitors. According to a report from the Combating Terrorism Center at West Point, 85 percent of all terrorist victims are Muslims. The Muslim community, therefore, has good reason to ally with American interests to defeat extremists. Those who assert the most extreme definition of Sharia agree with the extremists' definitions of Islam and help create an environment of alienation and distrust—which serves extremist interests, not American interests.

Adopting the CSP's analysis—and the hysteria over the "Sharia threat" that it is clearly intended to provoke—will prevent us from working with our natural allies and weaken our ability to protect ourselves. The war against extremism cannot be labeled as a war against Islam. Taking such a civilizational, apocalyptic view could well become a self-fulfilling prophecy. Further, we actually allow extremists to operate more freely without a clear identification of the threat and a consistent and constitutionally defensible system for recognizing and tracking extremists.

It is important to recognize that Muslims are in an ongoing conversation to define what their faith will look like. They have engaged in that conversation for centuries. But the challenge of faith and modernity is not unique to Muslims, and we cannot single them out for their beliefs.

Finally, it's important to note that even if the most extreme interpretation of Sharia were the correct one, there is no evidence that the U.S. legal system is in any danger of adopting tenets of Sharia.

To put this in perspective, the extreme Christian right in America has been trying for decades to inscribe its view of America as a "Christian nation" into our laws. They have repeatedly failed in a country in which more than three-quarters of people identify as Christians.

It's extremely unlikely that an extreme faction of American Muslims, a faith community that constitutes approximately 1 percent of the U.S. population, would have more success. We need to both respect constitutional freedoms and understand that the Constitution and our courts guarantee a separation between church and state.

The "Sharia threat" argument is so irresponsible as to almost demand a comic response, were it not for the disastrous consequences of adopting it. It's important that its claims be interrogated rigorously, in order to understand that they should not be taken seriously.

Organizations to Contact

The editors have compiled the following list of organizations concerned with the issues debated in this book. The descriptions are derived from materials provided by the organizations. All have publications or information available for interested readers. The list was compiled on the date of publication of the present volume; the information provided here may change. Be aware that many organizations take several weeks or longer to respond to inquiries, so allow as much time as possible.

ACT! for America
PO Box 12765, Pensacola, FL   32591
(705) 739-5920
e-mail: info@actforamerica.org
website: www.actforamerica.org

Founded by Brigitte Gabriel, a Lebanese immigrant to the United States, ACT! for America is an advocacy organization whose mission is to oppose what it describes as the threat of radical Islam to the United States. Articles and information about the organization's current campaigns can be found on its website.

Center for American Progress (CAP)
1333 H St. NW, Floor 10, Washington, DC   20005
(202) 682-1611 • fax: (202) 682-1867
website: www.americanprogress.org

The Center for American Progress is a progressive think tank concerned with public policy. Since the fall of 2009, the Faith and Progressive Policy Initiative at CAP has been engaged in its Young Muslim American Voices Project, which attempts to lessen the gap between public misperceptions and the reality of Islam. Articles covering these topics and more can be found on the organization's website.

Center for Security Policy
1901 Pennsylvania Ave., Suite 201, Washington, DC   20006
(202) 835-9077 • fax: (202) 835-9066
e-mail: info@centerforsecuritypolicy.org
website: www.centerforsecuritypolicy.org

The Center for Security Policy is a conservative think tank concerned with issues of national security. The organization has a number of publications that warn of the threats of Islamic extremism and Sharia law, which it makes available on its website.

Center for Strategic and International Studies (CSIS)
1800 K St. NW, Washington, DC   20006
(202) 887-0200 • fax: (202) 775-3199
website: www.csis.org

The Center for Strategic and International Studies is a bipartisan nonprofit organization that conducts research and develops policy in the fields of defense and security policy, global problems, and regional studies. The center hosts the Congressional Forum on Islam to foster debate and discussion among scholars of Islam and government policymakers. In addition, CSIS publishes books such as *Modernization, Democracy, and Islam; Islam and Human Rights*; and *Islam, Europe's Second Religion*, which explore the impact of the religion worldwide. The *Washington Quarterly* is the official publication of CSIS.

Council on American-Islamic Relations (CAIR)
453 New Jersey Ave. SE, Washington, DC   20003
(202) 488-8787 • fax: (202) 488-0833
e-mail: info@cair.com
website: www.cair.com

The Council on American-Islamic Relations is an Islamic advocacy group "dedicated to providing an Islamic perspective on issues of importance to the American public." CAIR conducts research on the American Muslim community and releases annual reports as well as news releases and other information, which it makes available on its website.

Council on Foreign Relations (CFR)

The Harold Pratt House, 58 E 68th St., New York, NY   10065
(212) 434-9400 • fax: (212) 434-9800
website: www.cfr.org

The Council on Foreign Relations is a nonpartisan, membership organization that provides information on and interprets current US foreign policy issues through its backgrounders, roundtables and study groups, and reports. CFR does not take any official position on the issues; rather its publications seek to present balanced views and provide a starting point for continued debate. The council addresses a wide range of subjects relating to Islam in its publications, including such titles as *Islam in America, Islam: Governing Under Sharia, Middle East: Islam and Democracy*, and *Women in Islam*. *Foreign Affairs* is the bimonthly magazine published by the council.

Middle East Forum (MEF)

1500 Walnut St., Suite 1050, Philadelphia, PA   19102
(215) 546-5406 • fax: (215) 546-5409
e-mail: info@meforum.org
website: www.meforum.org

The Middle East Forum is a conservative think tank whose mission is to "promote US interests in the Middle East and protect the Constitutional order from Middle Eastern threats." The forum advocates for a policy that fights radical Islam, improves democratization efforts, and advances the study of the Middle East in the United States. Articles on the website are organized by topic, including Islam, Radical Islam, and Democracy and Islam. MEF's official publication is *Middle East Quarterly*.

Middle East Policy Council (MEPC)

1730 M St. NW, Suite 512, Washington, DC   20036
e-mail: info@mepc.org
website: www.mepc.org

The Middle East Policy Council is a think tank committed to enhancing the understanding of the political, economic, and cultural issues that affect US interests in the Middle East. Its mission is enacted in three ways: publishing the quarterly journal *Middle East Policy*, conducting the Capitol Hill Conference Series for policymakers and their staffs, and presenting professional development workshops for K-12 educators. Articles and events sponsored by the organization often focus on the relationship between current issues in the Middle East and Islam.

Minaret of Freedom Institute

4323 Rosedale Ave., Bethesda, MD   20814
(301) 907-0947
e-mail: mfi@minaret.org
website: www.minaret.org

The Minaret of Freedom Institute is an Islamic libertarian organization whose mission is to educate both Muslims and non-Muslims in order to promote greater understanding and acceptance between the two groups. For non-Muslims, the institute's goal is to counter misinformation about Islam by explaining the compatibility between Islam and modern values and to advance the status of Muslim people. For Muslims, the institute seeks to educate the community about the benefits of free markets and liberty and to promote free trade and justice as a common interest of both Islam and the West. Articles about Islamic society, women in Islam, civil liberties, and others can be found on the institute's website.

Muslim Council of Britain (MCB)

PO Box 57330, London   E1 2WJ
   United Kingdom
+44 (0) 845 262 6786 • fax: +44 (0) 207 247 7079
e-mail: admin@mcb.org.uk
website: www.mcb.org.uk

The Muslim Council of Britain is an umbrella organization for more than five hundred national, regional, and local organizations, mosques, charities, and schools. The council works to promote understanding of Islam through its publications, projects, and events. The MCB provides an online library of articles, fact sheets, and reports.

New York University Center for Dialogues:
Islamic World–US–The West
194 Mercer St., Floor 4, New York, NY   10012
(212) 998-8693 • fax: (212) 995-4091
email: info@centerfordialogues.org
website: www.islamuswest.org

Founded after the terrorist attacks of September 11, 2001, the Center for Dialogues seeks to foster communication among Islamic and American communities and the West in total. Conferences sponsored by the center focus on topics such as the clash of perceptions; Muslims in the West; and how the media and educational institutions shape perceptions. The center hosts conferences and publishes reports, which can be read on its website or downloaded.

Project on Middle East Democracy (POMED)
1611 Connecticut Ave. NW, Suite 300, Washington, DC   20009
(202) 828-9660
website: www.pomed.org

The Project on Middle East Democracy was founded to assess methods of developing democracies in the Middle East and to make recommendations for how the United States can foster this development. The organization publishes policy briefs, reports, and articles and makes them available on its website.

Washington Institute for Near East Policy
1828 L St. NW, Suite 1050, Washington, DC   20036
(202) 452-0650 • fax: (202) 223-5364
website: www.washingtoninstitute.org

The Washington Institute works to advance an understanding of US interests in the Middle East and promote the policies that advance them. Research areas focus on individual countries in the region as well as on larger issues such as US policy in the region and the impact of Islam on interactions between the Middle East and the West. Reports on these issues and others can be read on its website.

Bibliography

Books

Christopher Allen   *Islamophobia*. Farnham, United
                     Kingdom: Ashgate, 2010.

Juan Cole   *Engaging the Muslim World*. New
                     York: Palgrave Macmillan, 2009.

John L. Esposito   *Islamophobia: The Challenge of*
and Ibrahim   *Pluralism in the 21st Century*. New
Kalin, eds.   York: Oxford University Press, 2011.

Liz Fekete   *A Suitable Enemy: Racism, Migration
                     and Islamophobia in Europe*. London,
                     United Kingdom: Pluto Press, 2009.

Peter Gottschalk   *Islamophobia: Making Muslims the*
and Gabriel   *Enemy*. Lanham, MD: Rowman &
Greenberg   Littlefield, 2007.

Evelyn Leslie   *Islamophobia and the Question of*
Hamdon   *Muslim Identity: The Politics of
                     Difference and Solidarity*. Black Point,
                     Nova Scotia: Fernwood, 2010.

Marc Helbling,   *Islamophobia in the West: Measuring*
ed.   *and Explaining Individual Attitudes*.
                     Abingdon, United Kingdom:
                     Routledge, 2012.

Joe L. Kincheloe,   *Teaching Against Islamophobia*. New
Shirley R.   York: Peter Lang, 2010.
Steinberg, and
Christopher D.
Stonebanks, eds.

Nathan Lean *The Islamophobia Industry: How the Right Manufactures Fear of Muslims.* London, United Kingdom: Pluto Press, 2012.

Jonathan Lyons *Islam Through Western Eyes: From the Crusades to the War on Terrorism.* New York: Columbia University Press, 2012.

Mohamed Nimer, ed. *Islamophobia and Anti-Americanism: Causes and Remedies*, Beltsville, MD: Amana Publications, 2007.

S. Sayyid and AbdoolKarim Vakil, eds. *Thinking Through Islamophobia: Global Perspectives.* New York: Columbia University Press, 2011.

Stephen Sheehi *Islamophobia: the Ideological Campaign Against Muslims.* Atlanta, GA: Clarity Press, 2011.

Andrew Shryock, ed. *Islamophobia/Islamophilia: Beyond the Politics of Enemy and Friend.* Bloomington, IN: Indiana University Press, 2010.

Periodicals and Internet Sources

Engy Abdelkader "Islamophobic Bullying in Our Schools," *Huffington Post*, November 30, 2011. www.huffingtonpost.com.

Arches Quarterly "Islamophobia and Anti-Muslim Hatred: Causes & Remedies," vol. 4, no. 7, Winter 2010.

Peter Beinart — "America Has Disgraced Itself," *Daily Beast*, August 16, 2010. www.thedaily beast.com.

Daniel Burke — "Senate Hearing Looks at Muslim Rights, Harassment," *Christian Century*, March 29, 2011. www .christiancentury.org.

Economist — "Can Careless Talk Cost Lives? The Growth of Islamophobia," July 30, 2011. www.economist.com.

Abigail R. Esman — "The Firebombing of Charlie Hebdo and the Continuing Fight Against Radical Islam in the West," *Forbes*, November 8, 2011. www.forbes.com.

Bryan Fischer — "Our First Concession to Sharia Law: Slavery," RenewAmerica, October 14, 2011. www.renewamerica.com.

Samuel G. Freedman — "Waging a One-Man War on American Muslims," *New York Times*, December 16, 2011. www.nytimes .com.

Jonah Goldberg — "Radical Chic," *New York Post*, January 9, 2011. www.nypost.com.

David Horowitz and Daniel Luban, interviewed by Marc Tracy — "Islamophobia or Reality?" *Tablet Magazine*, August 27, 2010. www .tabletmag.com.

Human Rights First — "Islamophobia: 2007 Hate Crime Survey," 2007. www.humanrights first.org.

Jeff Jacoby | "The 'Islamophobia' Myth," *Boston Globe*, December 8, 2010. www .boston.com.

Ian Kershaw | "Ghosts of Fascists Past," *National Interest*, February 23, 2011. http:// nationalinterest.org.

Gema Martin-Munoz | "Unconscious Islamophobia," *Human Architecture: Journal of the Sociology of Self-Knowledge*, vol. 8, no. 2, Fall 2010.

Feisal Abdul Rauf | "Ground Zero and Islamophobia in America," *Washington Report on Middle East Affairs*, vol. 29, no. 8, November 2010.

David J. Rusin | "Where's the Islamophobia?" *Journal for the Study of Antisemitism*, vol. 2, no. 2, December 2010.

Stephen Schwartz | "Islamophobia: America's New Fear Industry," *Phi Kappa Phi Forum*, vol. 90, no. 3, Fall 2010.

Adam Serwer | "CPAC: Infiltrated by Radicals? Grover Norquist Takes on the Right's Islamophobic Conspiracy Theorists," *American Prospect*, March 2011. http://prospect.org.

Peter Skerry | "The Muslim-American Muddle," Brookings, Fall 2011. www.brookings .edu.

Robert Spencer   "Fear, Inc.: The Business of Saving
                      Jihad from 'Islamophobia,'" *Human
                      Events*, August 30, 2011.
                      www.humanevents.com.

Cynthia White   "Negotiating Muslim Youth Identity
Tindongan   in a Post-9/11 World," *High School
                      Journal*, vol. 95, no. 1, Fall 2011.

Hans von   "Sharia Law: Coming Soon to a
Spakovsky   Courtroom Near You," The Heritage
                      Foundation, November 21, 2010.
                      www.heritage.org.

Robert Wright   "Islamophobia and Homophobia,"
                      New York Times, October 26, 2010.
                      http://opinionator.blogs.nytimes.com.

Index

A

Abbas, Ibn, 169
Abdulmutallab, Umar Farouk, 107
ACT! for America, 41
Afghan National Army, 80
Afghanistan
  Islamophobia and, 17, 78, 144
  Muslim liberation in, 94
  Taliban in, 76, 78, 145, 151
  war in, 55–57, 66, 144
African Americans, 41, 45, 72, 77
Aftergood, Steven, 71–72
Ahmadinejad, Mahmoud, 187
Ahmed, Akbar, 73–74, 82–86
Ahmed, Ishtiaq, 158–159
Ahmed, Leila, 54–58
Al Qaeda
  9/11 attack by, 75, 99
  Islamic extremism and, 38
  against Muslims, 94
  Obama, Barack backing of, 135
  Park51 project, 97
  Taliban and, 76
  threat of, 36, 42, 144, 150, 183
Aladdin (film), 22
Al-Azhar University, 156, 168
Albigensian Crusade, 30
Al-Din wal-Siyasa (Religion and Politics) (al-Qaradawi), 132–133
Ali, Wajahat, 36–44, 194–202
Allen, Ron, 103
Amanpour, Christiane, 104
American Civil Liberties Union (ACLU), 71

American Enterprise Institute, 39, 184
American Family Association, 41
American Muslim Council, 95
American Muslims
  alienation of, 42–43
  court cases between, 175
  as dangerous, 51
  growing population of, 113
  Islamic practices of, 120–121
  Islamist radicalization of, 161
  mosque attendance by, 170–171
  no 9/11 backlash against, 89–100
  persecution of, 41, 50
  post-9/11 discrimination of, 65
  safeguarding of, 89–92
American Physical Society Committee on the International Freedom of Scientists, 70
American Thinker (magazine), 128
American University, 73
Amish, 112
Amman Message (2004), 198
Anchorage Charitable Fund, 39
An-Na'im, Abdullahi Ahmed, 60, 157
Anthrax mailings, 67
Anti-abortion ideology, 68
Anti-Arab Discrimination Committee, 95
Anti-Defamation League (ADL), 37, 97–98
Anti-Islam grassroots organizations, 39

M

T

U